Linn's
Philatelic Gems 2

All of stampdom's enticing rarities cannot be covered in one book. Hence, this *Philatelic Gems 2*. Many of the stamps and covers herein are no less scarce than the pinnacles of philately described in the first *Philatelic Gems*. These, too, are the best stamp collecting has to offer — a few of them even rarer than some detailed in the first *Gems*.

Welcome to the continuing romance and mystery of *Philatelic Gems 2*.

by
Donna O'Keefe

Published by *Linn's Stamp News*, the world's largest and most informative stamp newspaper, Post Office Box 29, Sidney, Ohio 45365. *Linn's* is a division of Amos Press, Inc., which also publishes the *Scott* catalogs and publications; *Coin World*, a weekly newspaper for the numismatic field; *Cars & Parts*, a monthly magazine for auto enthusiasts; and other publications for the stamp, coin and auto hobbies.

Third Printing
Copyright 1989 by Amos Press Inc.

400076   ISBN 0-940403-03-X

In Grateful Appreciation . . .

I wish to thank these dealers and collectors who helped make *Philatelic Gems II* a reality:

Willy Balasse
Alan Benjamin
John R. Boker, Jr.
Ted Bozarth
Bridger & Kay Ltd.
Peter Collins
Robert Cunliffe
David Feldman
Ed Fraser
Scott Gallagher
Keith Harmer
Dr. Norman S. Hubbard
Robson Lowe
Walter Mader
Louis K. Robbins
Peter Robertson
Robert A. Siegel
Herbert A. Trenchard
Scott Trepel
Patricia Stilwell Walker
W. Danforth Walker
William R. Weiss, Jr.
Ian W. Whyte

Donna O'Keefe

Contents

INTRODUCTION.	7
ARGENTINA	
1862 15-centavo tete-beche	9
AUSTRALIA	
1897 Lake Lefroy local.	11
1920 Ross Smith label	13
AUSTRIA	
1867 3-kreuzer color error	16
BARBADOS	
1878 1-penny bisect	18
BELGIUM	
1916-18 2.50-franc surcharge error	20
1920 65-centime Termonde invert	22
BRAZIL	
1930 5-reis Parahyba provisional	24
BRITISH CENTRAL AFRICA	
1907 Unissued 2- and 4-penny values	26
BRITISH HONDURAS	
1888 Unreadable 2-cent black surcharge	28
CANADA	
1851 New Carlisle provisional.	30
1899 Port Hood provisionals	32
CHILE	
1854 5-centavo litho stamps	34
CHINA	
1897 $1 small surcharge	36
1915 $2 Hall of Classics invert	39
CHINA (Communist)	
1968-71 Cultural Revolution rarities	41
COLOMBIA	
1919 Airmail serif error.	44

DOMINICA
1886 1-penny surcharge error................................ 46

EGYPT
1868 Suez Canal Company locals 48

FINLAND
1856 5- and 10-kopeck tete-beches........................ 50

FRANCE
1857 Gauthier Freres & Cie locals 53
1869 5-franc missing value 55
1870-71 Bordeaux 20-centime varieties 57
1928 Catapult mail inverted surcharges.................... 59

GERMANY
1849 Bavarian 1-kreuzer tete-beche........................ 62
1862 Baden Land Post stamps............................. 64
1862-65 Baden 3-kreuzer imperf............................ 66
1895 Bavarian Aichach provisional postage due............. 68

GOLD COAST
1883 1-penny on 4d provisional 69

GREAT BRITAIN
1840 House of Lords envelopes............................ 71
1867-82 Early high values 73
1870 "OP-PC" corner errors............................... 76
1870-76 Stock Exchange forgeries......................... 78
1902-04 Withdrawn Edward VII Officials.................... 80
1902-04 Board of Education Officials...................... 82
1935 2½-penny Prussian blue.............................. 84
1961 2½-penny missing black error 86

GRENADA
1875 1-penny rough-perf 15 88

HONDURAS
1925 Red Honduras airmail................................ 90

IRELAND
1922-23 Misprinted overprints 92
1935 2-penny Map of Ireland coil 95

ITALY
1851-52 Tuscany rare values 97
1861 Neapolitan unissued series 99
1861 Neapolitan color errors.............................. 101

LIBERIA
1941 Postponed flight airmail surcharges 103

MAURITIUS
1848-59 Post Paid impression varieties 105

MEXICO
1864 Hidalgo issues. 108

NATAL
1857 First embossed issues 110

NEW SOUTH WALES
1850 Rarest of the "Sydney Views". 112

NEW ZEALAND
1854-59 Chalon Heads 114

NIGER COAST
1892-94 Oil Rivers provisionals 116

NORTHERN NIGERIA
1904 25-pound high value 119

NOVA SCOTIA
1851 1-shilling violet types 121

PUERTO RICO
1898 Post-invasion Ponce provisional 123

REUNION
1852 Two ornamental first issues 125

RUSSIA
1857 Tiflis Town Post local 127

SPAIN
1851 5-real red-brown color error 129

SWEDEN
1879 Tretio "double-value" error 131

SWITZERLAND
1849-50 Geneva's transitional 4-centime 133

TONGA
1897 7½-penny inverted king error. 134

UNITED STATES
1845 New Haven provisional 136
1846 Providence provisionals 138

1851 1-cent blue Franklin varieties 141
1857-61 5-cent Type I Jefferson brick red 144
1861 Confederate Knoxville provisional 146
1861 The "August" issues 148
1861 Confederate Mt. Lebanon provisional 150
1861 Confederate Livingston provisional 152
1867 1-cent blue "Z" grill 154
1870-71 24-cent rare grill 156
1871 $500 "Persian Rug" revenue 158
1893 4-cent Columbian blue 160
1902 Full-face McKinley postal card 162

URUGUAY
1858 180-centavo vermilion color error 165

VANCOUVER ISLAND
1865 5-cent rose imperforate error 167

Introduction

Many collectors have been introduced to this wonderful hobby of ours through intriguing stories of the blind watchmaker creating the famous Mauritius "Post Office" issue. But few collectors are familiar with the story of the rare Mauritius "Post Paid" issues which succeeded the "Post Office" stamps.

Oddly enough, these frequently ignored "Post Paid" issues bring five-figure realizations when sold. An expensive issue whose story is seldom told.

Ask a collector what ranks as the world's rarest airmail stamp, and he undoubtedly will say the Black Honduras. But is he aware that this unique stamp has overshadowed another scarce airmail issue from the same country — the Red Honduras? Only seven copies of this stamp exist. Another forgotten rarity.

It is to these "underrated rarities" that this book is devoted. Those great stamps whose fascinating stories are seldom told.

An Italian state issued only eight stamps in its brief history. Nevertheless, it contributed several rarities to the list of "gems" of philately. One set of gems was never issued, but a few were stolen from the printer and have found their way into collectors' albums.

A postman gave his wife sheets of obsolete postmaster's provisionals. She papered their attic wall with the stamps. But when their son realized the potential value of the provisionals, he carefully removed them from the wall, even regumming a few.

After more than 1½ million postal cards picturing the assassinated U.S. President McKinley had been printed, the postmaster general ordered all of them destroyed. A box of 500 somehow escaped, to be used by a firm that dumped New York City's garbage at sea. Today, these "garbage cards" are the gems of U.S. postal stationery.

The 1851 12-penny black, 1868 2¢ green on laid paper and 1959 Seaway invert are recognized as Canada's greatest rarities. But far scarcer is the forgotten, yet unique, provisional issued for the Canadian town of New Carlisle. This second edition of *Philatelic Gems* introduces collectors to the many rare stamps and covers lurking in the overpowering shadows of the more famous 1856 British Guiana penny magenta and United States 1918 inverted Jennies.

Like their illustrious kin, these lesser known, yet expensive, rarities are out of reach of all but the wealthiest of collectors. But the legends of their creation and discoveries continue to entice collectors to this great hobby in hopes of someday finding that one-of-a-kind gem in a dark attic or dusty album.

These fascinating stories keep collectors' hopes alive — and the philatelic dream goes on . . .

ARGENTINA

A Tete-beche Pair

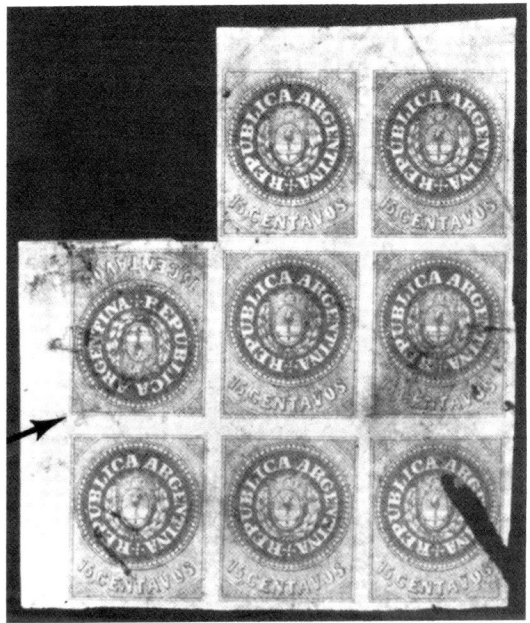

VALUE: $50,000 plus

Argentina's rarest philatelic item, the 15-centavo tete-beche pair of 1862 (arrow at lower left), is part of this block of eight from the Dale-Lichtenstein collection.

A careless printer created Argentina's rarest stamp by inserting a subject upside down in the printing plate. This resulted in a tete-beche pair. Very few of them exist.

The Argentine Confederation issued its first stamps May 1, 1858. In 1861 General Justo Jose de Urquiza and General Bartolome Mitre defeated Argentine President Santiago Derqui in a civil war.

General Mitre and General Urquiza then came to an agreement that Mitre would run the country; Urquiza would govern the provinces of Entre Rios and Corrientes.

Argentina was proclaimed a republic in 1862, and Mitre became its first constitutional president. Of course, the new republic needed stamps to reflect this change in its political status.

A local printer, R. Lange in Buenos Aires, lithographed the new stamps featuring the seal of the republic. Lange worked under primitive conditions. But, remarkably, few major errors occurred.

The 15-centavo denomination created the most trouble for Lange and his pressmen. This value is found with the accent missing on the "U," a variety which is valued at $8,000 unused and $4,000 used in Scott catalog.

However, Argentina's greatest philatelic rarity is the 15c tete-beche pair. The pressman accidently inserted one subject upside down in the printing plate. The inverted stamp occurs in the first position in the second row of the sheet.

Few of these tete-beche pairs exist. An irregular unused block of eight containing the error was auctioned in the Dale-Lichtenstein sale conducted by H.R. Harmer in 1969. Today, the tete-beche pair catalogs in Scott at $50,000 unused and $30,000 used.

AUSTRALIA

Lake Lefroy Bicycles

VALUE: INDETERMINABLE

This tete-beche pair, discovered in an old collection in London, was the first proof to philatelists that the Lake Lefroy locals were actually printed in tete-beche format.

The Blue Swan of Western Australia with the inverted center ranks as one of the world's scarcest postage stamps. Likewise, a stamp bearing a red swan ranks as one of the world's scarcest locals. This 6-penny local was issued for a bicycle mail service between the Western Australian goldfields of Lake Lefroy and Coolgardie, nearly 50 miles away.

In 1897 H. Lacey Hillier and Frederic E. Maskell introduced a private bicycle mail service between the two mining towns. Providing a mail service for prospectors, however, was not an original idea. James A. Healy had organized private bicycle and camel posts in Coolgardie as early as 1893.

However, his services were shut down by the Western Australia postal authorities because they infringed on the post office's monopoly of moving the mails. Lacey-Hillier and Maskell either were unaware of the post office's objections to infringements on its territories or they simply chose to ignore them.

In February 1897, the two men formed the Lake Lefroy Goldfield Cycle Mail. To indicate prepayment of postage, they issued 6d stamps printed in red on green wove paper and featuring Western Australia's famous swan.

The issue was printed from a zinc plate in sheets of four. Only 250 sheets (1,000 stamps) were produced, which accounts for their scarcity today. The zinc plate was defaced to prevent any reprinting of this issue.

In June 1897, Lacey-Hillier and Maskell were informed by the Western Australia postal authorities that their private mail service also violated postal regulations. They were ordered to cease operation or face the consequences. After the service was discontinued, a few copies of the unused stamps were sold to collectors. All remaining copies were destroyed.

In 1972 a remarkable discovery was made by a collector in London. He found a tete-beche pair of the Lake Lefroy local in an old collection. This was the first proof to philatelists that the locals were produced in tete-beche format.

Each Lake Lefroy local is perforated 12, and most bear the manuscript initials "H & M" (Hillier and Maskell) between parallel lines to guard against forgeries. The stamps were affixed to envelopes to be carried by bicycle between Lake Lefroy and Coolgardie. Of course, Western Australian stamps were required on any correspondence destined for areas outside the two towns.

AUSTRALIA

A Local or a Label?

VALUE: $1,540

This cover, bearing the label for the Ross Smith flight from England to Australia, was sent from Smith to his mother. The cover and enclosure realized $1,540 in a December 1984 Christie/Robson Lowe's sale.

Australia's Ross Smith label: Is it a local stamp, or is it merely a label? Stamp collectors disagree on this point. Whatever its status, this vignette realizes high prices when sold. At the December 12-13, 1984 Christie's/Robson Lowe auction, a cover bearing the label, along with a letter from aviator Ross Smith to his mother, was sold for $1,540.

As with many of the early airmail items, this label's story is tied in with an aviation competition. Thus, it joins the ranks of the Newfoundland airmail overprints and the United States Vin Fiz labels, as well as other aerial gems.

On March 19, 1919, the Australian Government offered a £10,000 prize to the first aviators to fly from England to Australia in 30 days or less. The flight had to be completed before December 31, 1920. The contest stipulated that the aviators must be Australian.

On November 12, 1919, Captain Ross Smith and his younger brother, Lieutenant Keith Smith, took off from Weybridge Airfield in Hounslow, England. Ross was the pilot; Keith the navigator.

The Smith brothers, along with two mechanics, landed their Vickers Vimy in Darwin, Australia, December 10. However, their final destination was Melbourne. They carried about 400 pieces of mail on the flight, and upon arriving in Darwin, Ross Smith sent a telegram to the Australian prime minister requesting a special stamp be issued to commemorate the historic flight.

It seems the prime minister and the aviator had two different concepts of the word "stamp." The prime minister immediately ordered a datestamp with the slogan "FIRST AERIAL MAIL-GREAT BRITAIN TO AUSTRALIA." What Smith had visualized was a commemorative postage stamp.

By the time Smith conveyed his idea to the prime minister, it was too late to prepare postage stamps. It is doubtful that commemoratives would have been prepared, even if there had been time.

Collectors disagree about the status of this issue. Is it a local stamp, or merely a commemorative label?

The prime minister compromised by ordering the printing of a commemorative label. This label was printed in dark blue by the Note Printing Branch. Crown over "A" watermarked paper was used. The format was similar to a perforated miniature sheet.

The design depicts maps of Britain and Australia with a torch in the center and a plane overhead. The inscription reads, "FIRST AERIAL POST/12 Nov-10 Dec 1919/ENGLAND-/AUSTRALIA."

Of the 576 stamps printed, 364 were affixed to the mail carried by the Smiths, 87 were given to the crew, and 125 supposedly were destroyed. However, Bill Hornadge, in his *Local Stamps of Australia*, says that in 1938, 22 unused sheetlets turned up in London. These once were owned by a man who was a government employee at the time of the flight.

The Smiths arrived in Melbourne February 25, 1920. The prime minister's department affixed the labels to the covers carried by the Smiths, canceled them with the special datestamp, and placed the covers in new envelopes. They then were sent to their various appropriate destinations.

Hornadge points out that since the prime minister took the mail from the official Australian mailstream, the label could be considered a local. It enabled the covers to get from the prime minister's office to the post office. However, most collectors still consider it only an official commemorative label.

This in no way diminishes interest in this scarce label. Collectors pay high prices to add a copy of this to their album pages. Those who cannot afford the genuine label, however, can obtain facsimiles produced by Philart Productions in England in 1969 and the A.S.A. Stamp Company in Adelaide in 1976.

AUSTRIA

From Green to Rose

VALUE: $25,000

Austria's 3-kreuzer color error of 1867 likely occurred when a 3kr cliche was inserted accidentally into a plate of 5kr rose-colored stamps.

Only five examples exist of a rare error on an Austrian stamp. This stamp is part of the 1867 series portraying Emperor Franz Josef facing right.

While the 3-kreuzer denomination of this series normally was printed in green and the 5kr in rose, this particular rarity is the 3kr in the rose color of the 5kr.

Collectors aren't certain how this spectacular error occurred. Some believe a complete sheet was printed in the wrong color. However, a more popular belief is that only one 3kr cliche was inserted in a plate of the 5kr. This more likely would account for the extreme scarcity of the error.

One of the five copies was owned by Count Ferrari, the great French collector whose stamps were sold following World War I.

The proceeds of that auction were credited to the German War Reparations Account.

However, when the Ferrari collection was sold, the 3kr rose error was unnoticed in a lot with other stamps, and the entire lot realized only a small sum. Another copy of the error also was in the famous collection of Arthur de Rothschild.

All examples of this rarity bear Hungarian postmarks, Hungary being a part of the Austro-Hungarian monarchy at that time. Also, the markings are dated in the same month, October.

For this reason, the Stanley Gibbons catalog lists the error under Hungary, since it is likely the stamp never was used in Austria. Scott, however, lists it under Austria with a price of $25,000.

The Unsevered Bisects

VALUE: $16,000
This unsevered pair of the Barbados 1-penny on 5-shilling bisect once rested in the albums of philatelists Alfred Caspary and Josiah Lilly.

Bisects always generate collector interest. Authorized use of a stamp cut in half is always fascinating, but an unsevered pair of a Barbados stamp originally intended for use as a bisect attracts particular attention. Some of the great philatelists have sought this pair. Alfred Caspary and Josiah Lilly were two who were successful in their attempts to own it.

In 1878 the tiny island of Barbados in the West Indies was in desperate need of 1-penny stamps. This was one of its most frequently used denominations, and supplies had run dangerously low. On the other hand, the post office had more 5-shilling Britannia stamps than it could use. So, the efficient postmaster decided to put these 5/- stamps to good use.

He created a provisional issue by ordering the bisecting of this denomination. The 5/- stamps were perforated down the center, and each half was surcharged with a numeral "1" (7 millimeters high) and a letter "D." (2¾mm high). The bottom label bearing the value "5 SHILLINGS" was cut off, so no blocks exist.

Two types of surcharges were used — slanting serif and straight serif. The slanting serif bisects catalog in Scott at $4,000 unused and $800 used. Much rarer is a mint unsevered pair of the slanting serif which is listed in Scott at $16,000. It is this pair that was owned by Caspary and Lilly. A used unsevered pair with straight serifs is now priced at $3,000.

   Unsevered horizontal pairs, imperforate between, exist with the slanting and straight serifs, but are not priced by Scott. The straight serif bisect is listed in Scott at $5,000 unused and $1,250 used. An unsevered pair catalogs at $4,250.

   A smaller surcharge was printed on the bisects later. The "1" is 6mm, and the "D." is 2½mm high. Again, an unsevered pair of this type is extremely rare, cataloging at $18,500 unused and $4,250 used. A number of varieties also exist with the surcharge reading either upward or downward.

BELGIUM

"2.50" Was Twice Too Much

VALUE: $4,750

All 13 known copies of the 2.50-franc on 1-mark Belgian occupation error were canceled at Charleroi.

    The Kingdom of Belgium was overrun by the Germans during World War I. The conquerors left their mark on everything in the country, including postage stamps. During the occupation, the German authorities ordered the overprinting and surcharging of German stamps to replace Belgian issues.

    Thousands of Germany's 1906-11 and 1916-18 stamps, showing Germania and allegorical designs, were overprinted "Belgien" and surcharged with denominations in francs and centimes.

    In his book, *Fabulous Stamps,* John W. Nicklin describes the discovery of Germany's "gift to Belgian philately" — a stamp which was incorrectly surcharged. Amidst the devastation of Belgium's many churches, libraries and public buildings, Antwerp's General Post Office remained standing, with records intact. Following the war, a philatelic researcher diligently examined the masses of correspondence and postal records in the post office.

Nicklin says the records indicated that the German 2-mark stamps had been overprinted and surcharged with a 2.50fr value for use in Belgium during the war. This was a well-known fact.

But the researcher also made a remarkable discovery in his studies. He found a 1m stamp with the same overprint and 2.50fr surcharge. The 1m stamps normally were surcharged with a 1.25fr value. The researcher had discovered an error.

Either during the overprinting and surcharging of the 2m stamps, a sheet of 1m was mistakenly run through the press, or the printer who was surcharging the 1m stamps forgot to change to the correct 1.25fr surcharge.

Most of the errors probably were used on correspondence and destroyed. Only 13 copies exist today. Each carries a Charleroi, Belgium, cancel dated June 18, 1917. The Scott catalog prices this surcharge error at $4,750.

Tipsy Town Hall

VALUE: $51,920

This pair of Belgian Termonde invert stamps represents one-eighth of all presently known copies.

The 65¢ Termonde stamp with inverted center is Belgium's own gem of philately and undoubtedly one of the rarest stamps of the world. Only 16 are known to exist.

The Belgian Post Office issued the Termonde stamp on August 5, 1920, to serve as a reminder of the great destruction that occurred during World War I.

The Germans leveled the city of Termonde, burning the houses and buildings, because city officials refused to pay a fine levied on them. The stamp depicts the beautiful Town Hall, which, of course, also was destroyed.

The 65¢ denomination was used for express letter service, or to pay combined registration and postage on foreign letters. Joh. Enschede & Sons in Haarlem printed only 5,000 sheets, each containing 25 stamps. These were delivered to the Belgian Post Office July 15, 1920, and distributed to various post offices throughout the country.

The stamps went on sale August 5 as planned. Eight days later, a clerk at the Ghent Central Post Office began breaking up a sheet in the normal manner to sell individual stamps to customers. Nine stamps from this sheet were sold to a hotel bellhop. Several other customers purchased the 65¢ stamps and affixed them to letters.

Then Hye de Crom purchased one of the Termonde stamps. He noticed something unusual about it. The Town Hall was upside down. The clerk had been selling stamps from a sheet with inverted centers without realizing it.

Knowing the potential value of these major errors, de Crom returned to the window to buy more stamps from the sheet. He succeeded in purchasing 16 inverts in all — the last three rows of the sheet and a copy from the first row. The other copies of this remarkable error probably were used on mail and later destroyed.

How did the error occur? Enschede printed the stamp in two stages — first the frame, then the center. On one sheet, the center was printed upside down in relation to the frame.

Willy Balasse, a famous collector and philatelic editor in Brussels, purchased a copy of the invert in the Josiah K. Lilly sale conducted by Robert A. Siegel Auction Galleries in 1967. He sold it to a collector in the United States, in whose collection it remains today. David Feldman SA sold a pair of the Termonde inverts at its October 24-27, 1984 auction in Zurich. The pair realized 130,000 Swiss francs (about $51,920). Scott catalog prices the invert at $4,000 either mint or used.

Additional copies of the 65¢ Termonde stamp were printed by the Malines Stamp Printing Office, this time in sheets of 100. No inverted centers occurred on this printing. However, these stamps were surcharged, and inverted surcharges have been found. But these in no way compare to the scarcity of the inverted centers.

The Rarest Zeppelin

VALUE: $16,000
Only 13 copies of the Brazil Parahyba provisional were produced, making it far scarcer than the famous U.S. 1918 24¢ inverted Jenny.

    The 1930 Europe-Pan America round-trip flight by the airship *Graf Zeppelin* was commemorated by more special stamps issued by various countries than any other airship flight.
    The *Graf Zeppelin* flew from Friedrichshafen, Germany, to Spain, Brazil, the United States, and back to Friedrichshafen from May 18 to June 6, 1930. Five countries issued 42 different stamps to prepay postage for mail carried aboard the airship on this flight.
    Elaborate arrangements also were made with Junkers planes in Germany and Condor planes in South America for connecting flights with the *Graf Zeppelin*.
    The scarcest of the stamps issued for this historic flight — the Brazil Parahyba provisional — was issued for the mail being carried to the airport for a connecting flight. This issue has failed to gain recognition by many of the major stamp catalogs. It is part of a quasi-official set of stamps issued by Brazil in 1930.
    Zeppelin officials, with permission of the Brazilian government, prepared 5,000-reis, 10,000r and 20,000r stamps that year featuring the *Graf Zeppelin* in flight over a boat at sea. The stamps carried the inscription "Primeiro Voo Commercial/Brasil-Europa."

Later, several of these stamps were overprinted "Graf Zeppelin/U.S.A." for mail carried to the United States. A shortage of the 5,000r and 10,000r also prompted the surcharging of the 20,000r denomination with these lower values. These stamps are fairly common and can be purchased at a nominal price. However, the gem of this set is the 20,000r surcharged "5" (reis) to prepay the local mail fee to the airport. Only 13 stamps received this surcharge, according to the Sieger *Zeppelin Post Katalog*. Of these, six are known on cover or card, one on piece, and two unused. An additional four covers should exist but have yet to be discovered.

Collectors refer to the 5r on 20,000r surcharge as the Parahyba provisional because it was used mainly in Parahyba, Brazil, although it also was posted at Recife. Of the two unused copies, one was offered in 1983 in a California auction. Experts examined this copy and concluded that it was reconstructed from parts of two stamps, one of which was not a "5" surcharge.

Therefore, only one sound unused copy exists. It has been authenticated by various experts, including Hermann Sieger, Francis Field and Arthur Falk.

When compared with the famous U.S. 1918 24¢ inverted Jenny, the Parahyba provisional is far scarcer. A full pane of 100 inverted Jennys was discovered. Yet, the U.S. inverts catalog in Scott at $110,000. The Parahyba provisional is not listed in Scott. Sieger catalogs the unused copy at 35,000m (approximately U.S. $10,560) and copies on cover at 50,000m ($15,090). The one sound copy of the provisional was auctioned in New York City April 27, 1985, by W.R. Weiss Jr. It realized $16,000.

BRITISH CENTRAL AFRICA

Right Country; Wrong Name

VALUE: $22,500 each

British Central Africa changed its name to Nyasaland before these stamps could be issued and distributed. They are now great rarities.

   The change in the name of a country resulted in what today are known as the rarest of King Edward VII British colonial issues. In the late 1800's and early 1900's, the British South Africa Company administered British Central Africa (now Malawi) under charter.
   At first, British Central Africa used Rhodesian stamps overprinted "B.C.A." However, the country began issuing its own stamps in 1895, a series featuring the colony's coat of arms.
   In 1903 British Central Africa introduced a new series portraying Britain's King Edward VII. The lower values were printed on watermarked crown and C.A. (Crown Agents) paper; the higher denominations appeared on crown C.C. (Crown Colony) paper.
   In 1907 Crown Agents, who coordinated the production of British Central Africa's stamps, introduced a new paper — multiple crown and C.A. They sent orders for new stamps on this paper to Thomas De La Rue and Company, printers in London. De La Rue immedi-

ately printed the 1-penny and 6d values and forwarded them to British Central Africa.

They then produced 2d and 4d values on the new paper. But before these could be shipped to British Central Africa, the colony changed its name to Nyasaland Protectorate.

What was to become of the 2d and 4d stamps bearing the old name? Crown Agents ordered the unissued stamps destroyed. Designs bearing the colony's new name were prepared.

However, years later stamp collectors discovered that not all the 2d and 4d had been destroyed. In 1918 Nevile Stocken purchased a mixture of Nyasaland stamps, which included 13 sets of the British Central Africa issue on multiple crown and C.A. paper. The mixture contained a multiple of ten, a pair, and a single of each of the four stamps.

In his book, *Stamps of Great Price*, Stocken recalled that he knew nothing of the 2d and 4d stamps when he discovered them in the mixture. His attempts to find information on the two values proved fruitless. Finally, he sold the entire mixture to a dealer, pricing the 2d and 4d at 10 shillings each. His copies were the only survivors.

Stocken later learned how foolish he had been. The stamps were great rarities. Scott catalog today lists singles at $22,500.

Only Red Could Be Read

VALUE: $14,000

British Honduras surcharged its 50¢ on 1-shilling stamps with "TWO" in black ink, but the black was barely visible on the gray stamps.

VALUE: $13,000

The printer handstamped British Honduras stamps bearing the "TWO" surcharge in black with a new, more readable surcharge in red.

British Honduras, now the Central American country of Belize, became a British colony in 1862. Four years later the colony introduced its first postage stamps. These stamps were typical of British colonial issues. They featured a portrait of Queen Victoria within an ornamental border.

In 1888 British Honduras changed its currency from British shillings and pence to dollars and cents. Of course, the colony needed to reflect this change on its stamps. The 1872-87 issues were surcharged with the new denominations in cents.

Still another problem faced postal officials in 1888 — a shortage of 2¢ stamps. The post office, therefore, ordered a second surcharging of the already surcharged stamps. Three different 2¢ surcharges were adopted: "2/CENTS;" "TWO;" and a more prominent and bolder "2/CENTS."

First, the printer surcharged the 50¢ on 1/- stamps with "TWO" in black ink. He immediately received complaints from the post office that the black ink was barely visible on the gray stamps.

The printer solved this problem by using red ink. To make certain the red ink worked, he handstamped the stamps, which already had been surcharged "TWO" in black, with the same surcharge in red. Stamps with the black surcharge and those with the black and red surcharges are extremely scarce. Only about ten each are known to exist in unused condition.

The black surcharged issues are listed in Scott catalog at $14,000 mint and $13,000 used. Those with the red and black are priced at $13,000 mint and $12,500 used.

The red handstamp proved to be a better choice, and many of these with a red surcharge only were issued. These stamps are common, cataloging $40 mint or used.

Arthur Hind, who compiled a fabulous worldwide collection, owned a mint copy of the black surcharge and a mint copy of the black and red surcharges. These were auctioned in the 1934 Hind sale by H.R. Harmer of London.

Canada's Princely Provisional

VALUE: $84,000

R.W. Kelly prepared this envelope with an impressed provisional stamp in 1851. Today, the New Carlisle provisional is Canada's greatest rarity.

Ask any collector what the rarest stamp of Canada is, and he is almost certain to mention either the 1851 12-penny black or the 1959 Seaway invert. He would be wrong. While these are the scarcest of the government issues, a little known provisional exists which is far rarer than all other issues of Canada.

This is the 3d provisional of New Carlisle. Stanley Gibbons catalog lists this stamp at £60,000 ($84,000). The 12d black is valued at $60,000 and the Seaway invert at approximately $18,000.

However, only one copy of the New Carlisle provisional exists, which accounts for its expensive price tag.

The provincial government of Canada authorized the prepayment of postage with stamps about April 1, 1851. R.W. Kelly, postmaster of New Carlisle, Gaspe, jumped the gun. He issued his own stamp on April 7 before supplies of the government's first stamps could reach the town.

Kelly's stamp was impressed in black on an envelope. It consisted of the words "Three Pence" within an ornamental frame. The only envelope bearing this impression is signed "Letter/R. W. Kelly/Apl 1851." It is addressed to Hugh Miller in Toronto and carries a New Carlisle-Gaspe April 7, 1851, postmark. Perhaps this is the only example of the New Carlisle provisional prepared by Kelly. It certainly is the only one to have been discovered so far.

Did Kelly create the provisional as an experiment, perhaps following in the path of the postmasters who issued provisionals in the United States? Was the provisional recognized by the Canadian government? These questions regarding Canada's greatest rarity remain unanswered.

CANADA

Stamps Split in Thirds

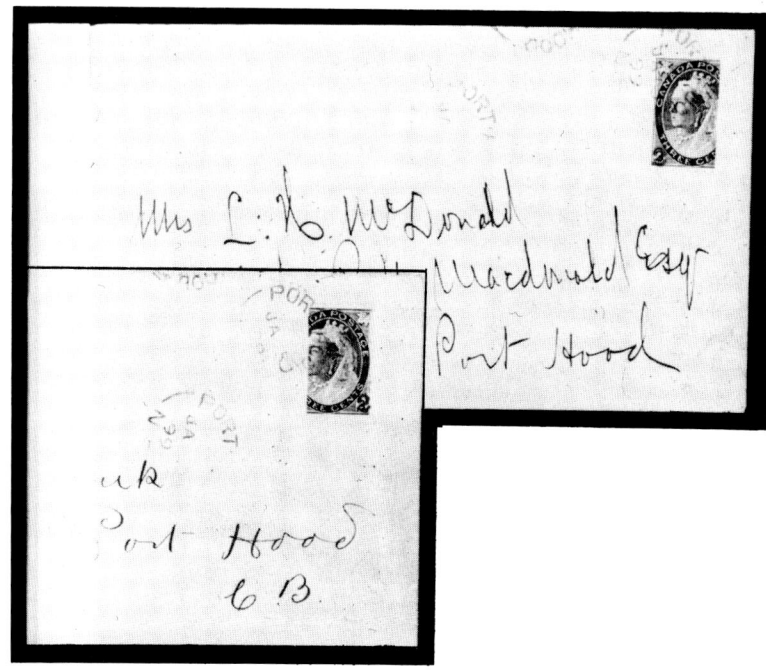

VALUE: $4,000

Two different portions of the 2¢ on 3¢ bisects of the Port Hood provisonal stamps appear on these locally addressed covers.

A change in postal rates and the fear of running short of stamps caused a postmaster in a small town in Nova Scotia to issue some unauthorized stamps — the Port Hood provisionals. These stamps now are very expensive, despite their having been declared illegal by the Canada Post Office.

The Stanley Gibbons catalog prices the 1¢ on 3¢ at £3,500 (about $4,600) and the 2¢ on 3¢ at £3,000 (about $4,000). Scott catalog lists the stamps, but offers no prices.

In January 1899, the Canada Post Office adopted a new rate of 2¢ for domestic mail. The postmaster in the small town of Port

Hood, Nova Scotia, panicked. His supply of 2¢ stamps was running short, and he knew he could not replenish them in time.

Without obtaining permission from the Canada Post Office, he took it upon himself to create his own provisionals. The postmaster used three sheets of 100 of the 1897-98 3¢ carmine stamps portraying Queen Victoria. He bisected the stamps vertically in unequal portions. He then handstamped a new value over the old — "2" in violet on the two-thirds portion, and "1" in blue on the remaining one-third portion.

The stamps were used January 5, 1899. However, when news reached the Halifax Post Office that the Port Hood postmaster was creating his own bisects, postal official Donald A. King sent inspector C.J. McDonald to investigate. The inspector confiscated all remaining bisects and destroyed them.

The Port Hood postmaster already had sold a few stamps and covers bearing the bisects to Stanley Gibbons prior to the arrival of McDonald. Today, these can be identified by the Gibbons name on the reverse sides of the stamps.

A few of the bisects saw local use, but most were used by the postmaster, who addressed covers franked with the bisects and sent them to his friends and local businesses. These bisects caused a furor at the Canada Post Office, but collectors continue to be fascinated by the peculiar provisionals and their history.

CHILE

Found in a Flea Market

VALUE: INDETERMINABLE

This cover, with its one-of-a-kind block of 14 5-centavo lithographed stamps, is one of Chile's most spectacular postal mementos.

A collector was rummaging through an assortment of covers at a flea market in Paris following World War II. In this unlikely location, he discovered one of Chile's great philatelic rarities. The collector came upon a cover bearing a block of 14 of the scarce 1854 5-centavo lithographed issue. Multiples larger than a strip of five of this stamp are rare.

The cover, addressed to Valparaiso, was later sold to John F. Rider, a New York collector. Rider's Chile collection was then sold intact to a New Jersey collector. Dr. Norman Hubbard is the present owner of the collection and the rare Chile cover.

But an enigma surrounds this 5c lithographed issue. Perkins, Bacon & Company, in London, engraved Chile's first 1853 issue. The set consisted of imperforate 5c and 10c values. Early in 1854, the post office experienced a shortage of stamps. Perkins, Bacon had shipped the plates and paper to Chile, so the post office enlisted a local printer to produce new stamps. N. Desmadryl, a Santiago printer, produced a beautifully engraved set from the Perkins, Bacon plates. The stamps were actually of finer quality than those from the London printer.

However, in 1890, A. Krassa discovered a pair of lithographed 5c stamps. He sold the pair to John N. Luff, who sent it to T.W. Hall in London for an explanation. Hall consulted with E.D. Bacon and other officials of Perkins, Bacon & Company, who concluded that the stamps were lithographic transfers taken from the first London plate produced for the 5c.

For years, these lithographed issues were attributed to another Santiago printer, H.C. Gillet. But today, most collectors believe this 5c also was printed by Desmadryl. The Stanley Gibbons South American specialized catalog lists Desmadryl as the printer.

But why would Desmadryl produce the cruder lithographed copies after he had printed such beautifully engraved stamps? Why did the post office order lithographed stamps when such perfection had been achieved through engravings? Was this an experiment? These questions still remain to be answered about this scarce issue of Chile.

But there is no question that the cover bearing the block of 14 of this issue is one of Chile's most spectacular philatelic items. Establishing a price is difficult because the cover in recent years has been sold as part of a collection.

A single copy of the 5c lithograph is priced in Scott catalog at $2,250 mint and $300 used. A pale brown variety is listed at $1,600 mint and $250 used.

Customary Greed

VALUE: $20,000
The 1897 $1 on 3¢ red revenue with its small, illegible surcharge became China's greatest stamp rarity.

China's 1897 $1 on 3¢ red revenue with its small surcharge ranks as that country's number 1 rarity. The provisional issue is listed in Scott catalog at $20,000.

In 1897 R.A. de Villard, a Chinese Customs postal official, walked up to the counter of a post office in China and purchased seven copies of the new stamp featuring the $1 surcharge.

He, along with other postal officials, had a jump on collectors. They knew the stamps with the small surcharges were being replaced immediately by those with larger surcharges. The small surcharges had proved too difficult to read. The cunning officials bought as many of the small surcharge issues as they could in hopes of cornering the market on what might become rare and valuable stamps.

De Villard kept a block of four intact. However, he died before he could tell anyone about his treasure. He bequeathed the block of four to his widow, a Chinese national.

M.D. Chow, who was putting together one of the great Chinese collections of all time, learned that Mrs. de Villard owned the block of four. He approached her several times offering to buy the stamps, but she refused to sell. Finally, in 1927, Chow convinced her to accept his offer. He paid a large sum of money for the block.

Chow later sold his rarity to Allen Gokson, a collector in the United States. Following Gokson's death, the block was sold to Lam Man Yin of Hong Kong. China's rarity returned to the Far East.

The $1 small surcharge on 3¢ red revenue is part of a series of provisional stamps issued by China in 1897 following the establishment of the National Post Office. Prior to this time, the mail was handled by the Customs Office.

With the debut of the National Post Office, the units of currency were changed from candareen, mace and tael to dollars and cents. New stamps were needed to reflect these changes. However, it was impossible to print new stamps in time for the new values, so the post office ordered the surcharging of all stamps in stock.

When supplies ran low, the post office also ordered the surcharging of the 3¢ red revenue stamps. These stamps had been printed as a means of collecting a tax, but the public outcry against the tax was so great that the Customs Office decided against it. The stamps were placed in storage. They were never used — at least not for revenue purposes.

When the post office became desperate for stamps, the revenues were surcharged with 1¢, 2¢, 4¢, $1 or $5 denominations, along with an Imperial Post overprint in Chinese characters.

The printing was halted after only a few sheets had received this small illegible surcharge. A larger surcharge was applied to the majority of the revenues.

Of the $1 small surcharge, less than 35 stamps exist today. Of these, the only block of four known to have survived is the one owned by Lam Man Yin.

Another block of four was broken up several years ago. Eugene Klein, the dealer who placed position numbers on the sheet of the famous U.S. 1918 24¢ airmail invert, owned three of the Chinese stamps from this surcharged revenue block.

He eventually divided the three stamps into a single and a horizontal pair because he failed to obtain a suitable price for the three stamps intact. He sold the single to Chow Tsu-peng and the pair to Saul Newbury, another famous U.S. collector.

Dr. James Senior later bought the pair. He separated it, says Huang Kwang-sheng in an article on the $1 small surcharge in the August 1982 *Postal Service Today*, the journal of the Republic of China (Taiwan) Postal Service.

An extremely rare variety occurs on the $1 small surcharge; it has no period after "dollar."

The surcharged revenue provisionals were superseded by a regular issue of stamps in August 1897. Thus, their term of duty was short-lived. In that short time, China's greatest rarity was born.

Chinese Checkered

VALUE: $4,800
This inverted center error on China's $2 Hall of Classics stamp occurred during a special printing in Peking.

A striking error occurred during the first printing in Peking of the China Hall of Classics $2 stamp. The stamp's center was accidentally turned upside down.

On May 5, 1913, China introduced a series of stamps whose basic designs, other than a few with revisions, remained in use for more than 20 years.

The first set was printed by Waterlow & Sons in London, and featured three designs and 19 denominations. The designs showed a Chinese junk, a farmer reaping rice, and the gateway of the Hall of Classics in Peking.

In 1915 China reissued the 19 stamps, but this time the Chinese Bureau of Engraving and Printing in Peking printed the set. These issues can be distinguished from the first printing by the perforations. The London printing is perforated 14 to 15, while the Peking productions are all perf 14.

A glaring error occurred during this Peking printing on the $2 denomination. The stamps were printed in two processes — first the frame and then the center. On just one sheet of 50, the center was accidentally inverted.

This sheet slipped by the postal inspectors at the printing office and was distributed for sale at post offices throughout China along with the normal stamps. However, a few copies survived.

The Scott *Standard Postage Stamp Catalogue* lists the inverted center error at $4,000 unused and $4,500 used. However, an unused copy realized 11,250 Swiss francs (about $4,800) at the October 19, 1983 auction of the Paul Hock China collection conducted by Robson Lowe/Christie's in Zurich, Switzerland.

CHINA (COMMUNIST)

Three Communist Miscues

VALUE: $4,500 plus
Three stamps produced by China during the Cultural Revolution have since become great rarities.

Three scarce and valuable stamps were produced by Mainland China (People's Republic) during the Cultural Revolution of the late 1960's and early 1970's.

The Cultural Revolution was the result of a clash over policy differences within the Chinese Communist party. Mao Tse-tung, China's head of state and chairman of the Communist party, joined the radicals on the mainland in their struggle to achieve a classless society. His regime promoted strict adherence to communist rules. Officials who failed to carry out party rules were ousted.

Many cultural figures, including historians and professors, were the targets of public attacks ordered by Mao and Lin Piao, China's minister of defense and Mao's heir apparent. Many universities and schools throughout China were closed in an attempt to create a new system of education which promoted this classless society. Violence erupted, and Mao called out the army to restore order. During this turbulent period, China issued three stamps with particular political significance. All three are now rarities.

The first was prepared to illustrate a strong political message; however, the designer failed in his attempt to please the ruling Communist party. The 8-fen stamp features a worker, farmer and soldier with the map of China overhead. The map is red, indicating that the entire nation was under communist rule.

Inadvertently, the designer showed Taiwan in white — a flagrant insult to communist officials on the mainland. Technically, the white Taiwan was correct. The defeated Nationalists fled to Taiwan (now the Republic of China) in 1949 and established their own one-party republican government.

But the communists on the mainland never have recognized this government and still consider Taiwan part of the mainland. To them, the island should have been shown in red.

The stamp was issued in November 1968, but when the white Taiwan was noticed, this issue was quickly removed from sale — only six hours after being released. Details about this stamp are sketchy because the United States had no diplomatic ties with China at that time. Communications between China and other countries also were almost nonexistent.

The stamp was placed on sale only at one post office in an obscure region of north China. Few copies exist. Scott catalog lists this stamp at $4,500 mint and $2,500 used.

Another stamp was issued in 1969 and withdrawn immediately. This 8f continued the series featuring Mao's thoughts, poems and writings. However, an observant person noticed an error in the inscription of the poem.

The stamp was withdrawn shortly after it went on sale. Used copies are scarce, but the great rarity is a mint copy, believed to be the only one to have survived.

Another 8f stamp was prepared in 1971 portraying Chairman Mao and Lin Piao. Chinese people are shown in the background, prominently displaying Mao's little communist red book. Just prior to the release of the stamp, Lin Piao and several other military officials mysteriously disappeared. So did the stamps.

Rumors floated around China that Lin had attempted to assassinate Mao. When he failed, he and his military accomplices tried to flee by plane. The plane crashed, killing everyone on board.

The stamp was never issued, although a few eventually found their way into the hands of collectors.

The Subtle Serif

VALUE: $7,000 plus

The stamp on the left of this pair shows the rare serif variety. The overprints were made for the Colombia Post Office's first airmail issues.

An American in Colombia was largely responsible for the creation of one of that South American country's most valuable stamps. In June 1919, Knox Martin, an American pilot, organized the first flight to carry mail in Colombia. Of course, Colombia had had no prior need for airmail stamps, and none was available to be affixed to the mail to be carried on the flight.

The Colombia Post Office, therefore, ordered the overprinting of two sheets of 100 of its 1917 2-centavo carmine rose definitives portraying Antonio Narino, leader of the Colombian revolutionary movement. However, the sheets were too large to fit on the overprinting press, so they were cut into strips of ten by guillotine. For this reason, the perforations are trimmed on most copies.

The stamps were overprinted one row at a time with the inscription "1er/Servicio/Postal/Aereo/6-18-19." All "1" numerals are sans-serif. However, the fifth stamp on each strip had the "1's" with serifs. Only 20 of this variety were produced.

Of the unused copies of the serif variety that exist today, two are in strips of three and three are in pairs. Scott catalog lists the normal overprinted stamp at $3,000 unused and $1,850 used. The scarce variety, however, is $7,000 unused and $4,000 used.

On June 18, 1919, Knox Martin flew his Farman biplane *Cartagena* from Barranguilla to Puerto Colombia, a short distance away. It seems, however, that Vicente Puccini, the postmaster of Puerto Colombia, should get some of the credit for this overprinted rarity.

Of the 160 covers flown, all but one are addressed to him or to his friend, Vicente Lombardi. The shrewd postmaster must have anticipated the future value of Colombia's first flown covers.

Only one nonphilatelic cover exists; it is in the British Museum. Martin's flight was so successful that Colombia's first commercial airlines, Compania Colombiana de Navegacion Aerea, was formed in Medallin later in 1919 to operate an internal mail service.

The Printer Goofed

VALUE: $27,500

Dominica's rarest stamp carries a 1-penny surcharge instead of the correct, intended ½-penny surcharge.

A shortage of stamps on the island of Dominica resulted in an interesting set of surcharged issues and the island's greatest rarity. In 1886 the Dominican post office ran short of ½-penny and 1d stamps. The island's stamps were printed in England.

There was no time to order a new shipment and wait for its arrival in the British colony. Stamps were needed immediately. Therefore, the postmaster in Dominica's capital of Roseau ordered the surcharging of 6d and 1-shilling values portraying Queen Victoria. The 6d received the ½d surcharge; the 1/- received the 1d surcharge. The original values were obliterated with a bar.

Although Dominica is the largest island in the Windward group of the West Indies, its printing facilities in the 1880's left much to be desired. It is not surprising that an error occurred; what is surprising is that only one occurred.

The printer surcharged a sheet of 60 of the 6d with the 1d denomination instead of the correct ½d. This error sheet was brought to the attention of a Mr. Porter, the treasurer of Dominica, in the late 1880's. Porter tore off a dozen of the 1d on 6d stamps and sent ten to A.C. Emerson, a friend in Great Britain who also was a stamp dealer.

In John W. Nicklin's *Famous Stamps*, he quotes Porter as writing to Emerson: ". . . There was a sheet of 6d green surcharged 'ONE PENNY' in error. Of these I have fortunately secured a dozen. I send them on an envelope to your address. Kindly return me the envelope entire after removing one stamp which will probably be acceptable for your collection and which you will oblige me by accepting . . ."

Porter eventually sold the stamps to Emerson for 5/- each. Today, Scott catalogs this error at $27,500 unused and $19,000 used.

Porter originally owned the only 12 error stamps known to exist. It is likely he ordered the other 48 destroyed.

EGYPT

A Short Life in Suez

VALUE: $44,800

The mixed franking of a French and a Suez Canal stamp makes this cover especially valuable and interesting to postal historians.

The short-lived postal service of the Suez Canal Company created fascinating stamps and scarce covers. Only 21 covers bearing these stamps exist.

Excavation of the Suez Canal in Egypt began April 25, 1859. Workers needed a postal service to carry their mail, so the Suez Canal Company established a private service in the isthmus. At first, the company charged no fees to move the mail between Port Said and Suez. But as the volume of mail increased, the company had to charge for this service to cover expenses.

Gustave Riche, general manager of the postal service, not only proposed charging fees for the conveyance of mail, but also suggested that the company issue its own postage stamps to indicate prepayment. Both proposals were adopted.

In April 1868, the company ordered stamps in four denominations from Messrs. Chezaud Aine et Tavernier in Paris. The denominations were 1 centime black, 5c green, 20c blue, and 40c red. The design features a ship with the inscription "CANAL MARITIME DE SUEZ." The values appear in the circles in the corners. The stamps were lithographed on paper watermarked "LA+-F," the abbreviation for Lacroix Freres, the paper producer.

The stamps were introduced in July 1868. However, when the Egyptian Post Office learned the company was charging fees to carry mail, it looked unfavorably upon the Suez postal service. The service was cutting into the Egyptian Post Office profits. The Egyptian Post Office terminated the Suez Canal Company's postal operations August 15, just a month after the stamps had been introduced. Egyptian issues replaced the Suez Canal stamps, and the Egyptian Post Office began carrying the mail.

Covers bearing the Suez Canal stamps are scarce. In their book, *Private Ship Letter Stamps of the World: Part 3, The Suez Canal Company,* Jean Boulad d'Humieres, S. Ringstrom and H.E. Tester describe and illustrate the 21 known covers.

One of the most interesting is the cover showing the earliest date of use, July 14, 1868. The cover, from Leon Labbe of Port Said, is addressed to Messrs. Mazet and Martin, merchants in Kantara. It is franked in the top left-hand corner with the 20c Suez Canal stamp, canceled by dots in a lozenge pattern.

Twelve of the covers bearing Suez Canal stamps, including this earliest-known-use item, carry the signature of Ap. N. Gennaropoulo in red ink on the back. Gennaropoulo was a collector living in Egypt. The Suez Canal book says he probably was an official of the Egyptian government. Eight of these 12 also carry the initials "M.G." in black or violet for Maurice Guiwelb, a London stamp dealer at the end of the 19th century.

A mourning cover addressed to Marseille is one of the most remarkable covers bearing the Suez Canal stamps. It is especially interesting to postal historians because it features mixed franking — a 20c Suez Canal stamp with a 40c French Empire issue. The 20c paid the Suez Canal Company postage from Ismailia to Suez; the 40c paid French postage from Suez to France. David Feldman sold this cover in his December 1, 1982 auction for 92,000 Swiss francs including 15 percent buyer's commission (about $44,800).

Two covers bearing the Suez Canal stamps are in the Royal Philatelic Collection at Buckingham Palace in London.

Finland's First Faux Pas

VALUE: $30,000

The first issue of Finland was printed so that tete-beche pairs were created. Shown is a tete-beche block of four of the 5-kopeck denomination. Arrows indicate secret markings found on the stamps.

Although Finland issued stamped envelopes in 1845, it was not until 1856 that it released its first adhesive stamps. These stamps have intrigued collectors because of their tete-beche pairs and secret markings.

The 5-kopeck blue and 10kop rose imperforate stamps made their debut in March 1856. They featured the same design used for the Finnish 1845 stamped envelopes, showing the coat of arms of Finland above two posthorns.

This issue was printed on a small press in the Stamp Printing

Office of the Finnish Treasury. The unwatermarked wove paper was inserted in the press to print the first row of ten stamps one at a time, and then turned upside down to produce the second row.

The result was that the rows were tete-beche (upside down) in relation to each other, creating the scarce tete-beche pairs for this issue. They are distinctive in that they seldom line up vertically.

Tete-beche pairs are priced in Scott catalog at $30,000 for the 5kop and $20,000 for the 10kop.

With the introduction of postage stamps, the Finnish Post Office changed its postal regulation, requiring the canceling of the stamp design. This was not done on the earlier postal stationery.

To distinguish the new stamps from earlier uncanceled cut squares of the postal stationery, pearls or colorless circles were inserted in the bell of each posthorn on the stamps.

To eliminate further confusion, the pearls also were added to all additional printings of postal stationery. The post office then allowed the public to use cut squares of the "pearl" printings of postal stationery on cover as postage stamps. Examples of such usage on cover are rare.

The Finnish Post Office instructed postmasters to cancel the new stamps, when affixed to letters, with their local postmarks. Post offices that handled mail and sold stamps also were given canceling devices. Since new postal handling procedures called for the dating of covers on mailing, a dated town canceler was included.

But the stamps frequently were canceled in ink, and sometimes precanceled before they were affixed to the cover. Occasionally, the ink-canceled stamps were canceled a second time with the dated town marking at the same post office.

It seems town cancels were only applied to the cover at the time of posting. Few covers exist bearing a town cancel applied as a transit cancel. Stamps bearing town cancels command higher prices than those with pen cancels.

On March 8, 1858, the 5kop blue denomination was issued with a slightly modified design. The pearls in the posthorns are larger, measuring 1mm in diameter, instead of .75mm.

The 50kop of the first issue catalogs in Scott at $7,000 mint and $1,200 used; the second issue is listed at $6,000 mint and $1,100 used. The tete-beche pair is priced at $30,000.

The 10kop of the first issue catalogs at $7,000 mint, $300 used.

Sometime in 1858, the 10kop with small pearls made its appearance on wide vertically laid paper. Scott lists this stamp at $1,100 used. The tete-beche pair is listed, but not priced. This issue's paper has 13 to 14 distinct lines per 2 centimeters. The stamp also exists on narrow laid paper, as does the 5kop with small pearls.

A 5kop large pearls variety was released in 1859 on wide vertically laid paper. This is one of the great rarities of this series. Scott lists it at $10,000 used or $12,500 with pen and town cancel.

Reprints of the 10kop small pearls and 5kop large pearls were released in 1862 on brownish vertically laid paper. Reprints also were issued in 1871, 1881 and 1893 on yellowish or white paper.

Stamps on diagonally laid paper are cut squares of stamped envelopes. Many of the stamped envelopes also were printed on wove paper.

Users of large quantities of postal stationery could have stamps imprinted on their own stationery. This is known as "printed to special order." Therefore, stamps that appear to be unwatermarked issues may actually be postal stationery cut squares. These stamps always should be expertized.

The quantities of stamps printed for the first issues were: 75,000 5kop small pearls, 547,000 10kop, and 125,000 5kop large pearls.

When these stamps were withdrawn, the Finnish Post Office was left with a combined total of 96,500 of the two 5kop stamps and 169,561 10kop. These unsold stamps were burned.

Steamship Locals Sunk

VALUE: $5,100

Only one entire bearing either the red or blue Gauthier Freres local exists. The stamp on cover is red, and the letter is addressed to Bordeaux.

The local stamps issued by Gauthier Freres & Cie are not only among the scarcest of all locals, they are also among the world's greatest philatelic rarities. Only eight stamps exist — seven red and one blue. The reason for their use of two colors always has puzzled collectors.

In the September 9, 1985 issue of *Linn's Stamp News*, noted philatelic writer L.N. Williams explained that in 1856-57 Gauthier Freres, a French-based steamship company, operated two services from Lyon — one between Le Havre and New York; the other between Le Havre and Rio de Janeiro.

The company issued local stamps to be applied to covers carried on the vessels. These oblong rectangular locals feature one of the Gauthier Freres ships, the *Barcelona*. The wording "Cie FRANCO-AMERICAINE/GAUTHIER FERES & Cie" surrounds the ship in an oval framework. The stamps are undenominated.

The scarcest item is a cover front bearing the only known copy of the blue stamp. It is addressed to Duarte Samaos & Ca. in Lisbon. The stamp is canceled "GMC" in blue. The cover also features the inscription "per *Franc Camtois*," another Gauthier Freres ship, and "4.10," the delivery charge assessed on arrival.

It was this piece that proved the authenticity of these locals. In 1877 C.H. Coster spread a veil of skepticism over these issues when, in his book *The United States Locals and Their History*, he said the company never existed. From then until the blue stamp was discovered early in the 20th century, collectors claimed the locals were bogus creations of American forger Samuel Allan Taylor. Although Taylor did create some Gauthier Freres forgeries, these eight stamps are genuine issues.

Only one entire exists. It is a letter from L. Seller in Rio de Janeiro to Monsieur Labunthe in Bordeaux. This entire sold for 13,500 francs (about $5,100) in the April 18, 1985 auction conducted by Christie's/Robson Lowe in Zurich. The piece bearing the unique blue stamp was offered, but found no buyers.

Another striking example is a vertical pair of the red local on a piece dated March 14, 1857, at Le Havre.

A disaster brought an end to the company and its services. In 1857, a Gauthier Freres ship, *Lyonnais*, was en route from New York to Le Havre when it was struck by the American ship, *Adriatic*. More than 100 persons were killed. The claims against the company were so damaging that it was forced out of business.

Williams points out that many forgeries of these locals exist. All genuine stamps bear a control marking, plus the script letters "GF & Co." in blue or black.

FRANCE

Napoleon of No Value

VALUE: $50,000

Count Phillippe von Ferrari's copy of the used France 1869 5-franc stamp with value omitted is shown at left. The normal stamp is seen at right.

The year 1869 was a banner year for stamps. In the United States, the Post Office Department issued its first pictorial set, which created the famous invert errors. The French Post Office introduced its first 5-franc denomination. An error also occurred on this issue, although its fame may not equal that of the U.S. inverts. This error is the 5fr with the value missing.

Following the victory of the armies of Napoleon III in Italy in 1861, the emperor, who was notorious for his vanity, ordered that his portrait be placed on all French coins and stamps with a laurel wreath denoting victory. However, the French Post Office had large stocks of old issues on hand, and the new stamps were not released until these were depleted.

The new stamps bearing the laureated head of Napoleon did not make their debut until 1863. Only two values were released that year — 2 centimes and 4c. The 10c, 20c and 30c were introduced in 1867; the 40c and 80c made their debut in 1868. The designs were similar to the rectangular stamps issued earlier, except for the emperor's laureated portrait.

In 1869 a need arose for a higher denomination. On November 1, 1869, the post office released a 5fr stamp. This covered the rate for franking heavier packages sent to foreign destinations.

This stamp differed in shape from the others. It was horizontal in format and twice as wide as the other stamps. The Napoleon portrait was the same as the one used for the other values.

The 5fr design carried the inscription "Empire Francais/Timbre Poste" in the border, and the value was printed with "5" to the left and "F" to the right of Napoleon's portrait. This stamp was printed in two separate operations. The background and portrait were produced in gray lilac. The value was applied in a separate printing, and appears to be in a slightly different shade. Because of these two operations, the position of the "5F" varies from sheet to sheet on this issue.

But a most spectacular error has the value missing completely. Only three specimens of this error exist. Two used copies are defective and carry Paris cancellations. An unused example of the error also has been recorded. A used copy was owned by Count Phillippe von Ferrari, the famous Frenchman whose collection in the early 1900's contained most of the great rarities of the world.

Collectors may ask why this stamp was printed in two separate operations. Surely, a second color was unnecessary for the value portion. Prudence was the answer. The French Post Office had contemplated issuing other high values. To save money in printing costs, the value was applied to the 5fr stamp in the form of an overprint. This enabled the printer to use the basic stamp design for other denominations without producing new plates.

It is this overprinting process which resulted in the differences in shade of the value from the rest of the stamp.

In the end, the French Post Office decided against releasing additional high values. A 1c denomination was added to the set in 1870, just before the entire issue was replaced by the Bordeaux stamps later that year.

The Franco-Prussian War broke out in 1870. Napoleon surrendered at Sedan in September of that year. The emperor was deposed and subsequently exiled. His portrait on French stamps was replaced by the goddess Ceres on the set of stamps known as the Bordeaux issue, because they were printed at the Bordeaux Mint during the siege of Paris.

The 1869 5fr bearing Napoleon's portrait remains one of France's most expensive stamps. Those with the value omitted are among her great rarities. The 5fr catalogs in Scott at $5,000 unused and $900 used. The stamp without the value is listed at $50,000 used.

Bordeaux's Color Errors

VALUE: $10,000 plus

Alfred Caspary once owned this horizontal pair of the 20-centime dark blue French Bordeaux-printed issue.

The siege of Paris during the 1870-1871 Franco-Prussian War cut off communication between the provinces and the French capital. The provinces also had no access to postage stamps being produced in Paris. So, a separate issue was prepared at the Bordeaux Mint almost simultaneously with the Paris printing. Two scarce varieties occurred among the Bordeaux printings.

The imperforate Bordeaux stamps featured the same Ceres design as the Paris printings. The scarce varieties occur on the 20-centime denomination. This denomination exists in three types.

Type I, produced from a woodcut by Dambourgez, has small inscriptions in the upper and lower labels, with a large space between the upper label and the circle containing the Ceres head. There is little shading under the eye and in the neck of Ceres.

Types II and III were engraved on stone by Leopold Yon. The inscriptions in the labels in type II are similar to those of type I, but the shading under the eye and in the neck is heavier. The upper label and circle almost touch.

The inscriptions in the labels in type III are much larger than those on the other two types. They are similar to the inscriptions of the other values in this set.

The rare varieties are differences in color shades. The 20c type I variety is in dark blue ink on bluish paper rather than the lighter blue on bluish. Alfred Caspary owned a horizontal pair of this rarity. The pair was sold in 1957 for $4,000 by H.R. Harmer, Inc. Scott catalog lists a single at $10,000 mint and $800 used.

The second scarce variety is the 20c type II in ultramarine instead of blue. Caspary also owned a cover bearing this stamp. It sold for $280. Scott prices a single at $15,000 mint and $3,000 used.

The type II stamp also is known in dark blue, but this is not nearly as scarce as the ultramarine variety. It catalogs at $1,050 mint and $100 used. An ultramarine variety of the 20c type III exists. Scott prices it at $2,000 mint and $675 used. When the siege of Paris ended in May 1871, the Bordeaux stamps were withdrawn, and the Paris issue was placed in general use throughout France.

France's Upside Down Airmail

VALUE: $10,000

This 90-centime stamp of France, with the inverted 10-franc Ile de France airmail surcharge, is one of the nation's scarcest issues.

France's greatest airmail rarities were the result of an experimental flight. But this was no ordinary flight; the plane was catapulted from the deck of the French Line flagship, *Ile de France*.

Ile de France plied the Atlantic between Le Havre, France, and New York, carrying passengers, mail and other cargo. A normal journey took six or seven days. In an effort to save time in the delivery of the mail, French Line officials decided to experiment with delivery by a seaplane carried aboard the ship.

When *Ile de France* left Le Havre August 8, 1928, arrangements were made to have the mail placed on board the seaplane piloted by Lieutenant Louis Demougeot. Anxious to participate in this experiment, the passengers inundated the ship's post office with letters to be flown on the seaplane.

The fee for the catapult service was 10 francs, and the supply of stamps with this denomination quickly was exhausted. No special stamps or cachets were applied to this mail; only the postmarks identify the covers as being carried on this first experimental flight. When *Ile de France* was 400 miles off the coast of New York, on August 13, the seaplane was catapulted from the deck of the ship. It made the flight in four hours, landing safely in Quarantine, New York, a day ahead of the ship. French Line planned a similar experiment for the return voyage, and passengers again prepared covers for a second catapult flight.

However, since the supply of 10fr stamps was depleted during the first trip, the ship's chief postal agent, Jules Cohen, decided to overprint the 90-centime and 1.50fr stamps he had in stock. He asked Maxime Mangendre, the French consul general in New York, to authorize the overprinting of the 10fr surcharge on the 90c Berthelot and 1.50fr Pasteur issues. Mangendre gave permission.

Cohen then contacted Emile Cabella of the French Printing and Publishing Corporation in New York, who applied the black "10FR." surcharge to the stamps by letterpress. Two black bars obliterated the original values.

The stamps arrived in time for the sailing on August 17. Of the 3,000 90c surcharged, 1,135 were used; of the 1,000 1.50fr, 250 were used. Only the ship's post office sold the stamps, and only a few philatelists were aware they existed prior to the ship's departure from New York. By then, it was too late to prepare covers.

Cabella overprinted the stamps in panes of 50, and one pane was discovered with the surcharge upside down. These invert errors were sold aboard the ship, with about 35 going to the crew.

Several varieties have been discovered, perhaps the most famous being the wide space between the "10" and the bars. This was intentional. On all five stamps of the ninth horizontal row, the space between the "10" and the bars is 6½ millimeters rather than the normal 4½mm. The printer changed this spacing so that the bars on the bottom row would cover the original values.

Scott catalog lists the inverted surcharge at $10,000 mint and used. The 6½mm space varieties catalog at $2,750 mint and used for the Berthelot, and $10,000 each for the Pasteur. Other varieties also exist, including a smaller "R" in "FR" on 11 stamps in each pane, and a broken foot "R" which occurs once per pane.

Some of the covers carried on the return journey received a handstamped cachet indicating that the mail had been carried on the catapult flight. Not all covers received this cachet, but all genuine covers should bear the August 23, octagonal "NEW YORK AU HAVRE" cancellation.

When the liner *Ile de France* was one day from the coast of France, the seaplane again was catapulted from the deck. When the French minister of posts and telegraphs learned of the provisional surcharge, he seized the remaining stamps and reprimanded Jules Cohen.

The French Post Office burned the confiscated stamps. According to E.H. Wilson's "The 'Ile de France' Provisional," which appeared in the July 1958 *Airpost Journal*, the number of surcharged stamps destroyed was 364 of the Berthelot issue. This means the stamps sold but never used totaled 1,501 of the Berthelot and 750 of the Pasteur.

Forgeries exist of this issue. A Philatelic Foundation *Analysis Leaflet* for the Ile de France provisionals indicates that of 59 Berthelot stamps submitted from 1945 to June 1980, 37 were genuine, and of 66 Pasteur issues, 28 were genuine.

The Ile de France stamps also hold the distinction of being the first issued and sold in the United States by a foreign government.

GERMANY

Inadvertently Tete-beche

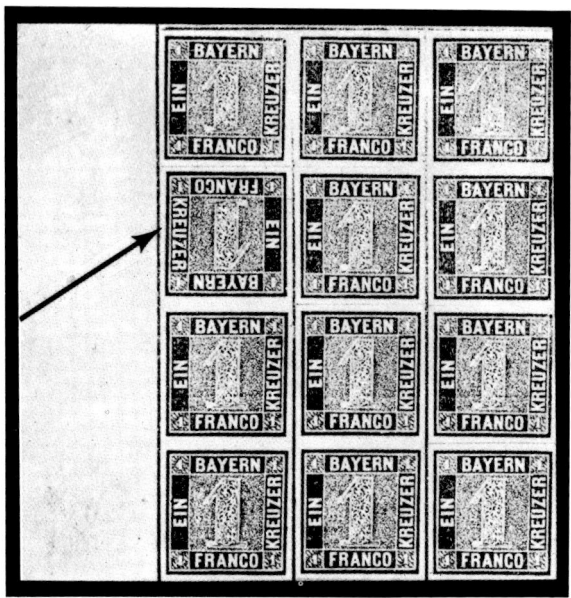

VALUE: $40,000

The tete-beche stamp is first in the second row of this block of 12 of Bavaria's 1849 1-kreuzer black.

Bavaria's first issue — the 1-kreuzer black of 1849 — is an expensive and desirable stamp, cataloging in Scott at $850 mint and $1,600 used. Tete-beche copies of this issue are another matter. Only three exist, all in mint condition. Scott lists them at $40,000, and even if you're one of the fortunate and wealthy collectors who has enough money to pay such a dear price, the tete-beche copies seldom come on the market.

Bavaria was the first of the German states to issue postage stamps. Its first issue consisted of three values — 1kr black for local letters and printed matter, 3kr blue for single letters weighing up to 1 loth (about one-third of an ounce), and 6kr brown for heavier letters and for those carried long distances.

P. Haseney prepared the simple designs which feature a large double-line numeral of the appropriate value. The numeral of the 1kr is decorated with arabesques and set in a square frame. The 3kr and 6kr show circular frames set against a field of solid color.

F.J. Seitz of Munich engraved the stamps. However, when it came time for J.G. Weiss to print these issues, the 1kr again became an exception. Its cliches were made from type metal; those for the 3kr and 6kr were struck in brass. Consequently, the 1kr stamps are not as sharp in detail as the other values. The type metal cliches wore down quickly.

The 1kr plate was arranged in ten horizontal rows of nine; the other two values in two panes, each containing nine rows of five. The 3kr and 6kr were printed on paper with silk threads to prevent forgeries. Only essays of the 1kr have paper with silk threads.

During the printing of the 1kr, however, something occurred which ensured that collectors for years to come would think of this stamp whenever Bavaria was mentioned. The printer unknowingly created tete-beche copies. (A tete-beche is a stamp printed upside down in relation to the other stamps in the sheet.)

Only three tete-beche examples exist, and surprisingly, each is from a different plate position. A block of 12 has a tete-beche as the first stamp in the second row. The famous French collector, Count Ferrari, once owned this block. Another block of 12 has the tete-beche as the first stamp in the fourth row. A block of 15 has the tete-beche in position 10 of the upper left pane.

Counterfeits of Bavaria's first issue exist, so collectors should have these stamps expertized. Of course, if you're offered a tete-beche version, be extremely wary.

Bavaria continued to issue its own regular stamps until 1920, longer than any other German state. (Wurttemberg issued Official stamps as late as 1923 but ceased issuing regular stamps in 1900.)

A few of Bavaria's stamps are extremely rare, cataloging up to $20,000. But none surpasses the tete-beche issues.

GERMANY

Baden's Double-Duty Stamp

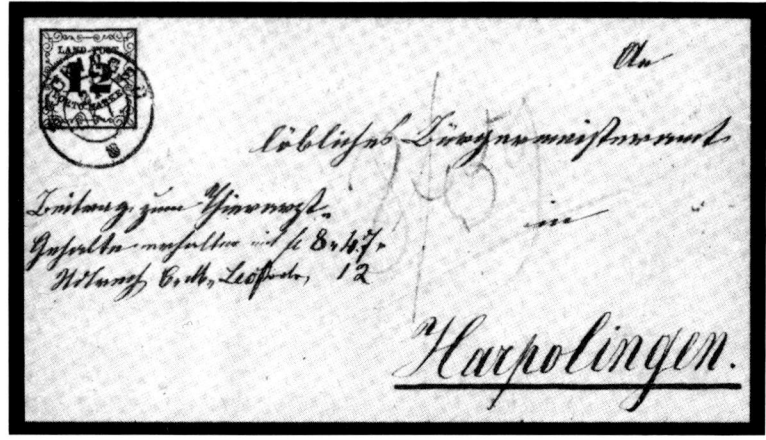

VALUE: $72,335

This Baden cover bears the 12-kreuzer stamp, used as a postage due.

The Land Post rural postage due stamps of Baden are fascinating issues. Unless you are familiar with the German States stamps, it is difficult to determine who issued these postage dues. No country name appears on the stamps, and the inscription "Land Post" is confusing. At first glance, they appear to be labels. But they're not. In fact, one denomination of Land Post issues ranks as one of Germany's greatest rarities.

The Baden postal authorities issued the rural postage dues in 1862 in three values — 1 kreuzer, 3kr, and 12kr. The postal authorities affixed these stamps to rural mail on which extra charges were payable by the recipient. These charges, however, did not strictly apply to postage due fees.

The stamps also were affixed when extra charges were payable for outstanding accounts, taxes, district funds, etc.

The stamps were not sold to the public during the nine years they were in use. The 1kr and 3kr denominations are relatively common, although used copies bring considerably higher prices than unused. Used copies of the 12kr are extremely rare. Scott catalog lists used copies at $15,000, compared with $45 for unused stamps of this denomination.

What makes the 12kr so rare? This value was used most often on money orders for the district funds of Walshut. The money orders were for large amounts, and the stamp saw little use. Only about 40 used specimens of the 12kr exist. Those actually used as postage dues are truly scarce.

A cover bearing a copy of the 12kr used as a postage due was auctioned in Berlin December 8, 1984, by Walter Kruschel for the astounding price of 230,000 marks (about $72,335). This rare cover was mailed by the mayor's office in Saeckingen to Harpolingen on October 21, 1869.

It first was sold by the German auctioneer, Heinrich Kohler, in 1927. At that time, Kohler claimed it was the only known cover with the 12kr postage due. In 1927, it brought 6,000m. When it was resold in 1929, it realized 7,700m.

Bisects also exist of the 12kr. Covers bearing half of this stamp used as a 6kr are listed in Scott at $22,500. Those bearing a quarter of the 12kr used as a 3kr catalog for $8,000.

Because used Baden Land Post stamps are worth much more than unused copies, forged cancellations abound. This is especially true of the 12kr.

Germany's First Imperfs

VALUE: $90,000

The Baden Stockach error has the distinction of being the first imperforate error in German stamp history.

The first imperforate error to occur in German philately is the rare Baden 3-kreuzer rose of the 1862-65 series. Only 18 copies of this error exist. All are used and canceled at Stockach between December 24 and 29. No year date appears on the cancel.

A copy of this error realized 240,000 Deutsche mark (about $90,000), plus buyer's premium, at the April 13-14, 1984 auction conducted by Walter Kruschel in Berlin. A collector in Germany purchased the stamp.

The German state of Baden issued its first postage stamps in 1851. They featured a numeral design and were imperforate. Baden issued its first perforated stamps in 1860. The post office changed the design for these first perforated issues, adopting the state's coat of arms for the central motif.

Hasper Printing Works purchased the perforating device in Austria. This device also was used to perforate the Wurttemberg stamps of this period. Baden's first perforated issues gauged 13½, but this proved to be unsatisfactory. Copies of the stamps with perfs intact are scarce, bringing higher prices than normal stamps.

The perforating device was later repaired and changed to a wider gauge, perf 10. When Baden issued the stamps with the new gauge in 1862, it also introduced another coat of arms design. Each value bearing this new arms design was perf 10, except the 3kr, which continued to be perf 13½.

Later in 1862, another 3kr denomination was issued perf 10. It was during the perforating of this stamp that the error occurred. A few sheets slipped through the perforating device without being properly perforated. Stamps that are entirely or partially imperf came from these sheets.

Of course, the entirely imperf copies are the great rarities. Because of their common cancels, collectors have nicknamed them the Stockach errors.

GERMANY

Because of One Hour's Delay

VALUE: $25,000 plus
The rare Aichach provisional postage due appeared because a telegram arrived just an hour too late.

A telegram failed to arrive at a Bavarian post office on time, resulting in the release of a stamp which never should have been issued. In 1895 a need arose in Bavaria for 2-pfennig postage due stamps. The Bavarian Post Office ordered the printing of stamps in this denomination, but later feared they might not arrive in time to meet the urgent need.

For the interim period, they ordered the surcharging of the 3pf gray postage dues with a 2pf value. The 3pf stamps were regular 1876 Bavarian issues already overprinted "Vom Empfanger zahlbar" (payable by the addressee) in red. The numeral "3" in each corner was surcharged "2" in red for the provisional issue.

Suprisingly, the new 2pf stamps arrived in time, so there was no need for the provisional postage dues. The Bavarian Post Office immediately sent a telegram to all local post offices advising them not to use the surcharged stamps.

The telegram arrived in time at all post offices, except one — Aichach. The Aichach postmaster began using the surcharged stamps. An hour later, he received the telegram and a supply of the new 2pf postage dues.

Obeying the order, he immediately withdrew the issue; and the surcharged stamps were destroyed. Only three used pairs of the Aichach provisional have been recorded.

Scott catalog places a $25,000 price on this short-lived stamp.

A Stamp Beyond Price

VALUE: INDETERMINABLE

Thomas K. Tapling owned this copy of the Gold Coast 1-penny on 4d provisional. It is now part of the Tapling collection in the British Museum.

Some of the world's greatest rarities can only be speculated upon by philatelists. So little information exists about them that collectors often doubt their legitimacy.

Gold Coast's 1-penny on 4d magenta of 1883 is one of the world's scarcest provisionals, but collectors continue to question its status. Most stamp catalogs carry statements to this effect.

This provisional stamp made its debut in May 1883, when the post office in Gold Coast experienced a shortage of 1d stamps. Supplies of the 4d red violet portraying Queen Victoria were handstamped "1D" in small type in black. The stamp saw limited use, probably for only a few days.

The only official mention of this provisional appeared in the *Philatelic Record* of June 1883, when a postal representative of the Gold Coast Post Office acknowledged that the stamp was authorized. Philatelists rely on this statement to prove its authenticity.

Another mystery surrounding this issue concerns the number of copies which still exist. Only one has been confirmed, and it is in the Thomas K. Tapling collection in the British Museum in London. The stamp is in used condition.

Rumors have circulated concerning a second example of the provisional. The famous philatelist Count Phillippe von Ferrari supposedly owned it, but the stamp was not in his collection when it was sold following World War I. If a second copy exists, its whereabouts are unknown at present.

Although most major catalogs list this rare provisional, they do not price it. How do you price a stamp when only one exists and it rests, untraded, in a museum?

An Envelope for Milord

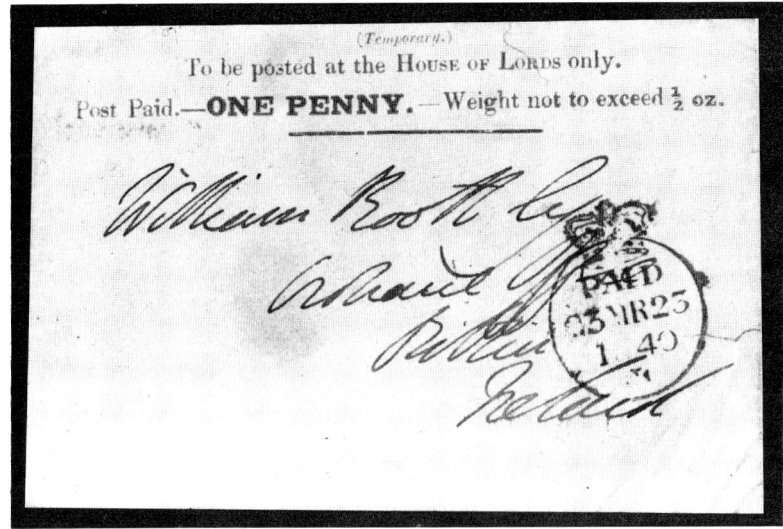

VALUE: $7,650

Britain's Parliamentary envelopes are among the world's scarcest postal stationery. The House of Lords issues are the scarcest of these gems.

Parliamentary envelopes rank among the world's most valuable postal stationery. They have the distinction of being Great Britain's first Officials, preceding the famous Mulreadys by four months.

Parliamentary envelopes also represented a victory for the common people, who bore the burden of high postal rates because government officials abused their franking privileges.

The British Post Office permitted members of Parliament to mail letters free just by signing the envelope or lettersheet. However, members took advantage of this perquisite for many years. They frequently gave friends stationery bearing their signature so their friends would not have to pay for postage. This cost the British Post Office thousands of pounds in revenue each year and drove postal rates up for the mailing public.

Rowland Hill suggested that the Post Office introduce a uniform penny postal rate. He said this low rate would increase the volume of mail by encouraging more people to send more letters. This would result in greater revenue for the Post Office and would ultimately justify the reduced rates. He also suggested that the free-franking privilege be abolished.

The Post Office adopted Hill's uniform penny postage proposal. It also abolished the franking privilege for members of Parliament on January 9, 1840, one day before the penny rate went into effect.

When Parliament reconvened on January 16 of that year, the Post Office provided members with special prepaid envelopes for official use at no charge. Although these envelopes did not carry imprinted stamps, the appropriate denomination was indicated in the inscription on the front.

The Houses of Parliament issues were released in 1 penny and 2d denominations, both printed in black. Only six of the 2d are in private hands, although a few are in museums.

The scarcest of the parliamentary issues are the House of Lords envelopes, which also were released in 1d and 2d denominations. The 1d shown here was addressed by the Duke of Wellington to the manager of his Irish estates. A 2d House of Lords envelope is in the Royal Collection. A 1d House of Commons envelope also was issued. This is the most common of the three issues.

An indication of the status of these envelopes was the word "Temporary" which appeared at the top of the House of Lords envelopes. The parliamentary envelopes were used only until the British Post Office introduced its adhesive stamps and Mulready postal stationery in May 1840.

This short period of use accounts for the envelopes' rarity. The Gibbons catalog values indicate their scarcity. The House of Lords issues catalog from £4,000 to £6,000 (approximately $5,100 to $7,650). The House of Parliament envelopes are listed at £1,250 ($1,600); the House of Commons issue catalogs for £750 ($950).

Britain's High-Value Rarities

VALUE: $30,000

Britain's first 1-pound stamp was issued on September 26, 1878.

VALUE: $22,500

This 10-shilling stamp of Great Britain is scarce in mint condition.

VALUE: $7,000

The British Post Office merely altered the printing plate for its 5-pound Telegraph stamp to produce this 1882 high-value stamp.

VALUE: $2,750

Great Britain released its first high-denomination stamp July 1, 1867.

Great Britain's early high-value stamps were prompted by necessity and now rank among the country's most valuable issues. The first high value, and also the most common in this series, is the 5-shilling stamp, which made its debut July 1, 1867.

The British Post Office received many complaints from large businesses demanding postage stamps in larger denominations. Too many smaller denomination stamps were needed to make the postage rate on some packages; barely enough room remained for the recipient's address.

The Post Office responded to mailers' requests by issuing the 5/- portraying Queen Victoria. The stamp was printed in rose in sheets of 80 on paper watermarked with the Maltese Cross. The design also features the check letters in the four corners and the plate number below the portrait.

The Scott catalog lists the 5/- at $2,750 mint and $150 used, so most collectors can afford at least a used copy of this issue. More expensive is the 5/- pale rose variety, listed at $3,000 mint and $140 used. Imperforate copies are cataloged at $4,000 mint (plate 1), and $3,750 mint and $180 used (plate 2).

On September 26, 1878, the British Post Office introduced 10/- and 1-pound high values. Both are extremely rare in mint condition — the 10/- listing at $22,500 and the £1 at $30,000 in Scott. Once again, used copies are more affordable, cataloging at $900 and $1,600, respectively.

These stamps also portray Queen Victoria, but their frames differ from each other and from the 5/-. They are similar in one respect: They continue to use the check letters, and they include the plate numbers in the designs.

Only one plate was made for the 10/- and £1 values. Like the 5/-, they were printed in sheets of 80. The 10/- was printed in slate and the £1 in brown lilac, both on Maltese Cross watermarked paper.

A fourth high value was introduced March 21, 1882. Its design differs tremendously from the other three stamps. This £5 issue is horizontal in format with the portrait of the queen in the center. The British Post Office altered the plate for the £5 Telegraph issue and substituted the word "POSTAGE." The stamp was printed in sheets of 56 on paper watermarked with two anchors.

Scott lists this issue at $7,000 mint and $2,000 used on white paper. A pale dull orange variety on bluish paper is listed at $20,000 mint and $2,600 used. A later printing in bright orange on bluish paper catalogs at $12,500 mint and $2,100 used.

Later, in 1882, the British Post Office decided to print its first high-value issues on a bluish safety paper with an anchor watermark. The 5/- made its appearance November 25, 1882; the £1 was issued a month later. However, the 10/- was not released until February 1883. The 5/- of this printing is the most common; the £1 is the scarcest. The stamps also are found on white paper.

Scott catalogs the set as follows: 5/- rose on bluish $8,000 mint, $700 used, with the same prices for the stamp on white paper; 10/- slate on bluish $25,000 mint, $1,400 used, and on white $27,500 mint and $1,500 used; and £1 on bluish $32,500 mint, $2,500 used, and on white $35,000 mint, $2,500 used.

As can be seen by their catalog prices, all these high values are scarce in mint condition; used copies are expensive but obtainable. Copies of the first issues of the 10/- and £1 stamps were auctioned in the Louise Boyd Dale sale by H.R. Harmer in 1969.

GREAT BRITAIN

When Two "C's" Made an "O"

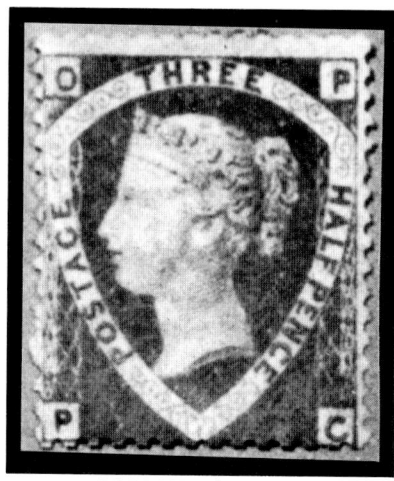

VALUE: $4,250

The engraver punched a correctly positioned "C" over an inverted "C," creating the mislettered "OP-PC" error of Great Britain.

An unusual error occurred on Great Britain's 1860-70 1½-penny issue. Some of the stamps are inscribed "OP-PC" in the corners instead of the correct "CP-PC." The stamp features a profile of Queen Victoria facing left with the inscription, "THREE HALF-PENCE POSTAGE."

Like many early British issues, the stamp carries letters in its four corners. Getting combinations of these letters correctly placed made forgeries more difficult. Each stamp on each plate had a different quartet of letters than any other on the same plate.

The 1½d denomination was first printed in 1860 in rosy-mauve color. The stamp was intended to meet a proposed increase in the postage rate for newspapers. However, in an unprecedented move, the British Parliament rejected the proposal for a rate increase. Of the 10,000 sheets of 1½d stamps printed, 8,962 sheets were destroyed. Each sheet contained 240 stamps.

In 1870 the 1½d rate was finally imposed. New stamps were printed from the old plates used to print the 1860 1½d stamps. This time, the printer used rose-red ink instead of rosy mauve.

In 1894 a collector discovered one of the stamps with the corner letters "OP-PC" instead of the correct "CP-PC." The error occurred on the third stamp (row C) in the 16th row (P). The engraver had mistakenly punched an inverted "C" in the top left corner of the stamp. He tried to correct his error by punching an upright "C" on top of the inverted letter. The result was a letter "O."

An imprimatur (proof) sheet is in the Reginald M. Phillips collection in the British National Postal Museum in London. It shows that the "O" actually was made up of two "C's" punched together.

All but one of the "OP-PC" errors occur on the rose-red stamps. These are scarce, but the true gem is a copy of the error in its original rosy mauve. The rosy mauve stamp was part of the 1860 printing. It is in the Royal Collection at Buckingham Palace.

The Phillips collection has an unused block of nine of the 1½d rose-red stamps, with the third stamp in the second row of the block showing the "OP-PC" error. The collection also has single used and mint copies of this variety. Scott catalog prices the "OP-PC" error at $4,250 mint and $700 used.

GREAT BRITAIN

The Forger Who Got Away

VALUE: $1,440

Stock Exchange forgeries are found on old British telegraph forms. They were not discovered until more than 25 years after they were created to defraud the British Post Office.

It is not often that a stamp forgery can be considered a gem, but the British Stock Exchange forgeries must be classified as such. After all, they represent the most famous of all British stamp frauds.

The British Post Office took complete control of the telegraph offices in Britain in 1870. Prior to the issuance of telegraph stamps by the Post Office in 1876, the charges were covered by the use of contemporary postage stamps. The initial rate was 1 shilling up to a maximum of 20 words, plus 3 pence for each five additional words. These stamps often were used on telegraph forms.

However, in 1898, a British stamp dealer, Charles Nissen, was examining his stock, which included several telegraph forms bearing copies of the British 1867 1/- stamps. He came across a few unusual copies. At first he could not determine what was wrong, but the stamps did not look right. Most were blurry.

Then he discovered one with an impossible combination of letters in the corners. He knew they must be forgeries. He reported his find to the postal officials, but more than 25 years had elapsed since the forgeries had been created. It was much too late to track down the culprit.

Although the forger has never been identified, he has been recorded in history as the creator of probably the only British forgeries to defraud the Post Office. Collectors should note that this forgery was created to bilk the Post Office, not philatelists.

It is believed that a clerk at the British Post Office probably forged the stamps to cheat the Post Office out of revenue from the telegraph service. He probably accepted the money for the stamps from the sender, but affixed the forgery instead of the genuine 1/- stamps. Thus, he was able to pocket the money without depleting his accountable stock of genuine stamps.

The forgeries were typographed singly on unwatermarked paper. They are not as sharp in appearance as the genuine stamps, and those from plate 5 are more crude than those of plate 6. All are canceled with the Stock Exchange Post Office marking from which they received their name. A November 27, 1980 auction conducted by Harmers of London featured several copies of the forgeries. These realized from £90 to £600 (approximately $216 to $1,440).

Several examples are now part of the Reginald M. Phillips Collection in the British National Postal Museum, London, England.

GREAT BRITAIN

Official for a Day

VALUE: $100,000
Great Britain's rarest Official was in use for only a few hours.

VALUE: $32,500
The 10-shilling King Edward VII I.R. Official issue is also a scarce item.

The British Post Office issued an Official stamp May 14, 1904 — then, on the same day, ordered all Officials withdrawn from use, thereby creating one of Britain's rarest stamps.

The post office began issuing Inland Revenue Officials in 1882, overprinting current issues "I.R./OFFICIAL." These stamps were used by the British department that handled revenue matters. Beginning in 1902, the post office began overprinting stamps of the new king, Edward VII, for Official use. Several of these are scarce.

But on May 14, 1904, the post office created its choice Official. On that day, the 6-penny Edward VII I.R. Official was issued. And on the same day, just hours after the stamp's release, the post office issued an order withdrawing all Official stamps from use. The 6d Official was obsolete only a few hours after its release.

Few copies exist of the 6d Official. The British Royal Collection in London has a used single and an unused pair and single. A nearly complete sheet is in the National Postal Museum Collection. Ard-Mhusaeum Na h-Eireann in Dublin has an unused block of four.

A few copies are owned by collectors. Harmer, Rooke and Company auctioned an unused single for £3,200 at its November 27, 1964 sale, a high price at that time. Today, this rare Official is listed in Scott catalog at $100,000 unused. No price is given for used copies, which are also extremely scarce.

Other rarities in the 1902-04 Edward VII I.R. Official series are the 5 shillings at $7,500 unused and $2,750 used; the 10/-, $32,500 unused, $20,000 used; and the £1, $22,500 unused, $7,000 used.

The British Post Office allowed collectors to buy unused Official stamps for only a short time after they were first issued in 1882. The stamps then were withdrawn from public sale, and a law was passed making it illegal to buy or sell unused Officials. This legal maneuver contributed to the scarcity of the stamps.

In the August 1978 *Gibbons Stamp Monthly*, British philatelic writer L.N. Williams relates an anecdote told by Charles Nissen, a famous British stamp dealer. When the Official stamps were withdrawn from use, the British Post Office lifted its ban against buying and selling these stamps. Nissen acquired a few unused 10/- Edward VII I.R. Officials and sold them through the mail for £17 10/-.

Most of his customers were delighted with the opportunity to own one of these stamps, but a shortsighted collector returned his, saying the price was too steep. Little did he know that it would be a small price to pay for a stamp that now catalogs at $32,500.

Board of Education Officials

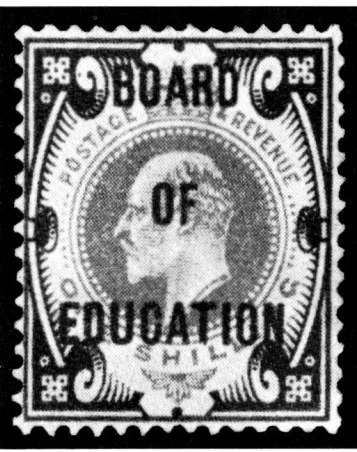

VALUE: $40,000
Britain's Board of Education 1 shilling Official is one of that country's greatest stamp rarities.

The 1-shilling value of Great Britain's Board of Education Officials is the most valuable stamp in this series, and the second most expensive of all British Officials. This may not sound too impressive. After all, Officials are relegated to the back of the book in most major stamp catalogs. They are given second-class status to regular and commemorative issues. But many of Great Britain's great rarities exist among these second-class citizens of the philatelic collecting world.

The 1902-04 6-penny I.R. (Inland Revenue) Official catalogs at $100,000; the unissued 1d black Official of 1840 lists at $11,000. And the Board of Education 1/- catalogs at $40,000 unused and $21,000 used — truly a great rarity.

The Board of Education Officials (also known as Departmentals) were issued by the British Post Office from 1902 to 1904 for use by members of the board. In 1902 Britain's 1887-92 5d and 1/- Queen Victoria regular stamps were overprinted "BOARD OF EDUCATION" in three lines by Thomas De La Rue and released by the British Post Office for use by this department.

Following the death of Queen Victoria and the coronation of King Edward VII, new regular stamps were issued portraying Britain's new monarch. The ½d, 1d, 2½d, 5d and 1/- denominations of this 1902-04 set also were overprinted by De La Rue for use by the Board of Education. At the time these Officials were in use, the public could not buy them in unused condition. Thus, unused copies of the Officials are scarce.

The Board of Education Officials were in use for only two years; in 1904 the British Post Office ordered the withdrawal of all Official stamps. This short lifespan also accounts for the stamps' scarcity.

While the 1/- Edward VII is the gem of this series, other values also are expensive. The 1/- Queen Victoria catalogs at $1,750 unused and $800 used. The 5d Edward VII is listed in Scott catalog at $2,250 unused and $750 used. Other Board of Education Officials are cataloged from $3.75 to $750.

GREAT BRITAIN

Britain's Prussian Blue King

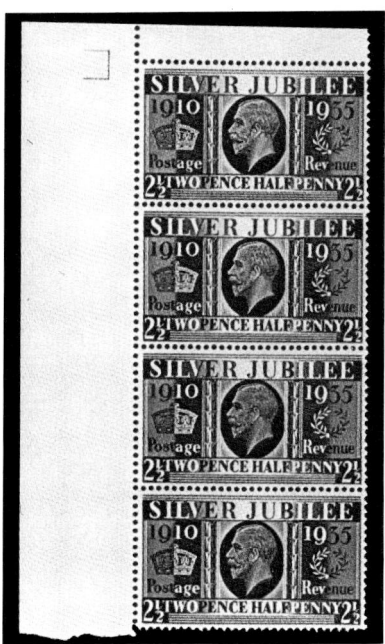

VALUE: $15,000
A collector purchased more than 300 rare Prussian Blue stamps at a post office in North Edmonton, London.

The Great Britain 1935 Silver Jubilee issue captures the attention of stamp collectors because it was the first British commemorative set to be printed by photogravure, and because the stamp designs were created by a famous contemporary artist, Barnett Freedman. However, the issue owes its fame more to the 2½-penny Prussian Blue than anything else.

On May 7, 1935, the British Post Office issued four stamps (½d, 1d, 1½d and 2½d) to commemorate the 25th anniversary of the accession of King George V to the British throne.

Barnett Freedman, whose paintings hung in Britain's most prestigious museums, including the Tate Gallery, designed the Silver

Jubilee stamps. The designs reproduced the MacKennal profile portrait of the king, with the crown to the left on each stamp and emblems on the right. The denominations and colors were ½d dark green, 1d carmine, 1½d red brown, and 2½d ultramarine.

One month after the stamps were released, a stamp collector bought copies of the 2½d at a post office in North Edmonton, London. He noticed their color was a greenish blue, different from other 2½d stamps he previously had purchased. This greenish blue shade now is referred to as Prussian Blue.

The collector asked the clerk if the post office had additional copies in this shade. The clerk said he had received three sheets of 120, but already had sold 41 from one sheet. Believing he may have stumbled upon a color variety, the collector bought the remaining 319 stamps.

He offered to sell these stamps to several dealers, but most hesitated to make him an offer. They were uncertain whether the stamps were varieties or simply part of a new printing. However, when no other copies were discovered, H. & A. Wallace, a London stamp dealer, purchased the bulk of the Prussian Blues. (The collector sent a few of the stamps to his friends.)

At first, it was believed the odd-colored stamps were color trial proofs rather than printing varieties. However, color trials were printed from a different cylinder producing stamps measuring 38.75 millimeters by 22.25mm. The Prussian Blues are the normal stamp size of 38.4mm by 22mm.

Stanley Gibbons catalog says the logical assumption is that the three sheets came from the beginning of a printing for which the wrong ink was used. When the error was discovered and corrected, the wrong color sheets somehow became mixed in with the regular supply rather than being destroyed.

The three sheets were perforated and delivered to the post office in North Edmonton. The unsuspecting clerk sold the Prussian Blues along with the regular 2½d stamps.

An imperforate sheet of the Prussian Blues is in the British National Postal Museum in London.

Scott catalogs these rare stamps at $6,000 unused and $5,500 used. An unmounted vertical strip of four realized £10,000 (about $15,000) in a 1981 Harmers of London auction.

GREAT BRITAIN

A Queen Loses Her Head

VALUE: $28,000

This block of British "missing black" stamps went unexhibited for 23 years.

A stunning mistake occurred on Great Britain's 1961 Post Office Savings Bank Centenary 2½-penny stamp. The stamp is missing the queen's head and the symbolic "thrift plant." This stamp was printed in red and black, but the black color is completely missing on the error.

A businessman in Rochester, Kent, England, purchased a block of stamps at his local post office in 1961. He immediately noticed that the queen's head and "thrift plant" were missing. All that remained was the white background where the queen's head should have been, along with the white inscriptions on a red stamp. The man tore one of the stamps from the block, placed it in his wallet, and gave the others to his secretary for safekeeping.

In 1963 rumors of the "missing head" variety spread throughout Great Britain. The businessman remembered placing a copy of the error in his wallet. He removed it, but by that time it was creased and soiled from being carried around for two years. He searched for the remaining copies from his block of stamps, but they had been discarded.

Bridger & Kay Ltd., noted British dealers and publishers, sold the man's single copy of the error at an October 2, 1975 auction. The battered stamp realized £325.

In 1984 B. Alan Ltd., a British dealer who specializes in varieties, sold a block of 15 of the Post Office Savings Bank issue. The company described the block of 15 as containing "six stamps missing the black completely and a further six with much of the black printing omitted." The three stamps at the right have small portions of the black missing. B. Alan Ltd. sold the block at the STAMPEX '84 show in Great Britain for £20,000 (about $28,000).

Although rumors of the existence of this block had circulated for many years, the first time it was exhibited was during the STAMPEX '84 show. At the time of its sale, Alan Benjamin, owner of B. Alan Ltd., declared this price to be the "highest ever paid for a modern British error." Scott catalog lists the "missing black" error but assigns it no price.

A "Hurry Up" Perf Job

VALUE: $8,000 plus
Only eight copies of this Grenada 1-penny stamp of 1875, perforated 15, have been recorded.

Check your Grenada 1875 1-penny stamps. If you have one perforated 15 with rough cut, irregular holes, you have a rarity. Scott catalog fails to list this stamp; however, Stanley Gibbons catalog does list it as No. 15.

This is the highest priced regular issue of Grenada, even though few collectors know about it. Only one unused copy has been recorded. It catalogs in Gibbons at more than $8,000. Seven used copies are recorded, including a horizontal strip of four and three singles. Gibbons lists the used stamps at more than $2,000 each.

The story of this rare Grenada stamp begins in 1872. Perkins, Bacon & Company of England printed Grenada's early stamps. In 1872 a 1d value in a distinct blue-green shade on large star watermarked paper was issued. This stamp has the star watermark sideways with two points of the star pointing to the top of the stamp. Previous issues of Grenada's stamps, as well as printings after 1875, were on unwatermarked or small star watermarked paper.

Again in August 1875, Perkins, Bacon printed another 1d green to yellow-green stamp on the large star watermark paper. However, in this printing, the star watermark is upright. This 1875 1d stamp was printed without difficulties, but problems arose in the perforating operation.

Until 1875 Perkins, Bacon also perforated Grenada's stamps. But the August 1875 printing of 1,020 sheets (120 stamps per sheet) of 1d stamps were sent to the British Board of Inland Revenue at Somerset House for perforating in October 1875. This perforation was a clean cut perf 14.

However, Somerset House botched part of their perforation job. Some have the perforations so misplaced that the gutter between the adjoining stamps is almost in the center of the perforations.

Perkins, Bacon was in a quandary. They had to deliver 1,000 sheets of the 1d stamps to fulfill their contract. On October 12, 1875, Somerset House supplied to Perkins, Bacon the 1,020 sheets they had perforated. One thousand sheets had to be sent to Grenada October 15. Perkins, Bacon found 60 of the sheets from Somerset House so badly perforated that they had to be scrapped.

With great haste, 40 new sheets were printed and perforated by Perkins, Bacon in four days. This printing was compatible with the August printing, but Perkins, Bacon used a different perforating machine than Somerset House. The stamps were perforated 15 with rough cut, irregular holes, rather than the clean cut perf 14 of the Somerset House perforated issues.

These perf 15 1d stamps are the rarities. Of the 4,800 1d stamps of 1875 with rough perf 15, only eight have been recorded. Others may exist, but most collectors are unaware of this perf 15 issue.

Check your 1875 1d Grenada stamps. The rarity has a large star upright watermark and rough 15-gauge perfs. This stamp is unknown to most collectors, but it is well worth a search.

The Rare Red Honduras

VALUE: $11,000

Only seven copies exist of this Red Honduras, although it continues to play second fiddle to its more famous sister, the Black Honduras.

Most collectors are familiar with the world's greatest airmail rarity — the Black Honduras. But few are aware that the Black Honduras has a sister stamp — the Red Honduras — which also ranks among the world's philatelic gems. Only seven copies of this stamp exist, which accounts for the high $11,000 price tag assigned to it by Scott catalog.

The Red Honduras is the 1915-16 Bonilla Theater stamp overprinted "AERO CORREO" in red and issued in 1925. In 1927 a block of seven of the Red Honduras was offered to Scott Stamp and Coin Company. The block of seven was broken into a block of four and three singles.

John Nicklin, a Scott employee, was given the task of selling the block of four and a single. This was no easy task. Few collectors were interested in stamps from the tiny country of Honduras, regardless of their rarity. Nicklin broke the block into four singles and sold them at a more modest price.

Today, collectors recognize the true value of this issue and are willing to pay high prices for genuine mint copies of the stamp. No used examples exist.

The story behind the Red Honduras is much the same as that of the Black Honduras. In the early 1920's, Dr. Thomas C. Pounds, an American living in Honduras, asked the Honduran government to issue special stamps to be used along with regular issues for airmail service on Central American Airlines, a new firm which he owned and operated. The service was to carry mail between Puerto Cortes and Tegucigalpa.

Plans were halted during a revolution in Honduras in 1923, but in 1925, the government sent Pounds a quantity of its 1915-16 definitives and gave him permission to overprint them. Dr. Pounds contracted with a local printer, Karl Snow, for the overprinting. Snow's facilities were limited; his overprints were careless and crude.

Snow's knowledge of the Spanish language also must have been negligible. The overprint reads "AERO CORREO" instead of the correct "CORREO AEREO." This overprint was applied in red, blue or black ink to the 5-centavo, 10c, 20c and 50c values. An "AERO CORREO 25" surcharge was applied in black or blue on the 2c, 5c, 10c and 20c stamps.

Snow overprinted blocks of 12 of these stamps; only one block of the red AERO CORREO overprint on the 5c light blue is believed to have been printed. Of these 12 stamps, only seven exist today.

IRELAND

Wrong Irish Accents

VALUE: $9,000

The "missing accent" error appears on the center stamp in this strip of Ireland's 1-shilling overprints.

VALUE: $7,000

This 1-penny copy is missing an accent and "t."

A printer, who was pressed for time, created Ireland's four greatest stamp rarities: the 1922-23 1-penny missing accent; 1-shilling missing accent; 1-penny missing accent and final "t;" and 10-shilling reversed accent inserted.

With the establishment of the Irish Free State in 1922, the Irish naturally wanted stamps to proclaim their country's new status. Selecting appropriate designs and printing new stamps took time, so the Irish postal authorities ordered the overprinting of some of Great Britain's George V issues.

The first series of overprints, issued in 1922, carried the inscription "Rialtas/Sealadac/na/h-Eireann/1922" (Provisional Government of Ireland).

However, Ireland's philatelic rarities belong to a later series of overprints — those carrying the inscription "Saorstat/Eireann/1922" (Irish Free State), with accent marks over the last "a" of "Saorstat" and the first "E" of "Eireann." These accent marks caused problems for the printer.

The overprints made their debut in December 1922 and January 1923, following the adoption of the constitution establishing the Irish Free State as a British dominion (self-governing country). An immediate demand arose for stamps carrying the new name. Postal authorities urged the printer, Alex. Thom and Company Ltd., to produce the overprints as quickly as possible.

But overprinting is never an easy task. The printer faces the problem of centering the overprint on sheets of stamps which already have been gummed and perforated. Time restrictions compound the problem. Errors are frequent, almost inevitable.

This was the situation with Ireland's "Saorstat/Eireann/1922" overprints. The printer created several varieties. During the overprinting, stamps were discovered with the accent missing over the second "a" of "Saorstat" in three positions. The missing accents occurred on the 12th stamp in the 15th row on plate I for the low values, and on the second stamp in rows three and eight for the high values.

Missing accent varieties have been discovered on the ½d, 1d, 2½d, 3d, 4d, 9d and 1/- of Britain's George V portrait stamps. They also can be found on the 2/6d, 5/-, and 10/- of the Britannia Rules the Waves issue.

While each of these varieties attracts collector interest, and while they range in Scott catalog value from $275 to $11,000, the 1d and 1/- missing accents surpass all others as gems of Irish philately. Another variety, the 1d with accent and final "t" of "Saorstat" missing, shares the limelight with these great rarities.

When the printer discovered the missing accents, he corrected the errors by inserting the accent by hand. However, this made matters worse. The inserted accent has been found reversed on some stamps. Particularly rare is the 10/- stamp with the reversed accent carelessly inserted.

Gerard Brady examined the provenances of recorded examples of the four rare overprint varieties in the winter 1978-79 issue of *Irish Stamp News* (No. 2), now published in Dublin by MacDonnell Whyte Ltd. Six years later, in the January-March 1984 issue (No.

17), Brady reported nine new discoveries of these varieties.

This serves as further proof that rarities still await discovery by collectors. Who knows what may lie undetected in that dusty stamp album in the attic?

Of the 1d missing accent, Brady listed six known copies, four mint and two used. Scott catalogs this variety at $10,000 mint or used. Nine examples are known of the 1/- missing accent, eight mint and one used. This rare variety is cataloged at $9,000 mint and $11,000 used.

Brady listed ten copies of the 1d missing accent and final "t" variety, six mint and four used. Prices are $7,000 mint or used.

Eleven copies of the 10/- reversed accent inserted variety have been recorded, ten mint and one used. This variety catalogs at $4,500 mint. Scott lists no price for the used copy. The 10/- also can be found with the missing accent. It catalogs $3,750 mint.

Although Ireland has issued stamps only for 63 years, it contributed these to the list of the world's great philatelic rarities.

Misperfed Map Coils

VALUE: $12,500
Ireland's most valuable stamp is this 1935 2-penny Map of Ireland coil, perforated 15 horizontally.

Ireland's highest priced stamp, the 2-penny Map coil perforated horizontally, received little attention from collectors until the 1950's, even though it was issued in 1935. This lack of interest among collectors contributed to the scarcity of the issue. Many were destroyed in the normal handling of correspondence. Collectors began noticing the variety in the 1950's, and the prices for copies of these have climbed steadily since.

The 2d perf 15 horizontally was issued as part of a coil series frequently referred to as Ireland's experimental coils. Whether these coils were intended for experimental use is subject to conjecture; nevertheless, they were in postal use for only a short time. This also contributed to the scarcity of the 2d variety.

The series consisted of ½d perf 14 vertically, 1d perf 15 horizontally with a variety showing a single perf at top, 2d perf 14 vertically, and the rare 2d perf 15 horizontally. The coil stamps were used in vending machines throughout Ireland, and also by such businesses as the Dublin Gas Company, Boileau & Boyd Ltd., and the National Assurance Company.

Mint copies of the 2d variety are exceptionally scarce. The earliest recorded mint example of this version was discovered by a collector in Ireland. He purchased it in an auction lot of coil stamps in the late 1930's.

In the summer 1981 issue of *Irish Stamp News*, published in Dublin by MacDonnell Whyte Ltd., Gerard Brady lists 20 known mint copies of this stamp. Particularly noteworthy is a vertical strip of five, the largest known mint multiple of this variety.

According to Brady, the strip was removed from a parcel by David Feldman and Bill Kane; thus, it is ungummed and creased. The strip is most spectacular since all five of the stamps are well centered. Most copies of this coil variety are off-center. Two mint vertical pairs also exist.

Used copies of the 2d coil variety are more common than mint copies, but they also sell for high prices.

Standard postage stamp catalogs failed to recognize the scarcity of this issue for many years. Stanley Gibbons first listed the variety in 1942, but without prices. Scott catalog first listed it in 1955, but again no prices were given.

A price of $75 for the used stamp was first included in the 1959 Scott catalog. A price for the mint stamp did not appear until the 1960 catalog, in which the stamp was listed at $150 mint and $75 used. Today's Scott catalogs price this rare variety at $12,500 mint and $1,400 used.

It is impossible to create the 2d variety by trimming the perforations from the regular 2d Map sheet stamp of 1922-23. The sheet stamp measures 20 millimeters; the coil variety 20.75mm. So, trimming the perforations results in a stamp that measures less than 20mm — an easily detected fake.

This is not to say that fakes do not exist. As with all rare stamps, collectors should have these Irish varieties expertized.

ITALY

Tuscany's Crazie Soldi

VALUE: $15,000 plus

This strip of three of the rare Tuscany 60-crazie stamp was once in the collections of Count Phillippe von Ferrari and Alfred Caspary.

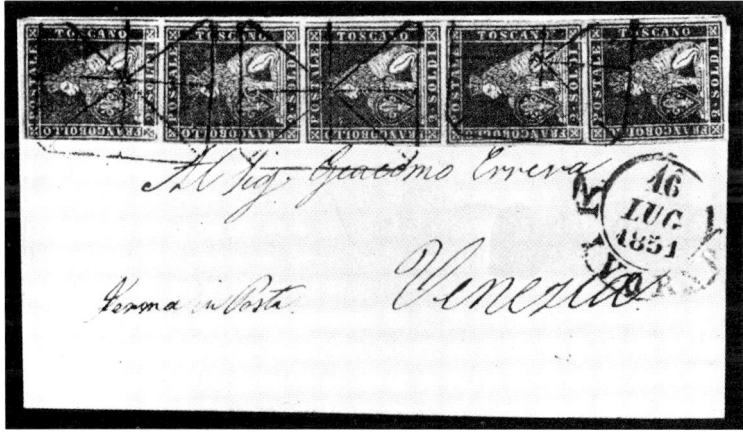

VALUE: INDETERMINABLE

This rare cover bears a vertical strip of five of the 1851-52 2-soldi stamp.

    The Italian state of Tuscany, famous for its 3-lira ocher rarity, also issued two other extremely scarce stamps. These two stamps — 2-soldi scarlet and 60-crazie red — were part of Tuscany's first issue released from 1851-52.

    The seated crowned Lion of Tuscany serves as the central design for this series of stamps. Although the other values appear on blue, grayish blue, or gray paper, the rare 2s and 60cr are found only on blue paper. The imperforate issues were typographed by the Grand Ducal Printing Office in Florence.

The 2s owes its scarcity to the fact the stamp was in use for only a short time. The stamp was placed on sale April 1, 1851, and was withdrawn in November 1852. The 60cr made its debut in November 1852. It was intended for use on weighty foreign correspondence. That very limited usage contributed to its scarcity.

Alfred Caspary, one of the great collectors of 19th century worldwide stamps and covers, owned a rare cover bearing a vertical strip of five of the 2s. The stamps are tied by a red "spider web" cancellation. The cover is postmarked Livorno July 26, 1851, and addressed and backstamped to Venice. At the 1957 auction of the Caspary collection by H.R. Harmer, Inc., this item realized $4,600. Caspary also owned a single, horizontal pairs, and a strip of three.

In addition to singles and pairs of the 60cr, Caspary once owned a strip of three of this rarity. The strip previously was in the Count Ferrari collection. At the Caspary auction, it realized $6,750.

Today, Scott catalog prices singles of the 2s at $8,000 mint and $2,250 used. The catalog lists the scarcer 60cr at $15,000 mint and $6,000 used.

ITALY

Stolen From a Printer

VALUE: $120,000

This cover bears the 10-centesimi stamp of a five-value Neapolitan Provinces set. But all values are rare, since the entire set was never issued.

Although the Neapolitan Provinces of Italy issued stamps for only a short period in 1861, the provinces contributed to the stamps considered "gems" by today's collectors.

Only one set of stamps was issued by the provinces. It was released in 1861 and replaced by stamps of Italy in 1862. However, a set was prepared by the post office of the Neapolitan Provinces but never issued. These stamps are extremely rare today. They closely resemble the series issued by Sardinia, another Italian state, from 1855 to 1861. The inscriptions on the Neapolitan issues have clearer and larger lettering than those of Sardinia. They portray King Victor Emmanuel II.

The provincial post office ordered the Neapolitan stamps printed in values of 5 centesimi, 10c, 20c, 40c and 80c, but the director of posts decided not to issue them. However, a few sets were stolen from the printer and used on correspondence. Only 13 used copies have been discovered.

These rare stamps so closely resemble the relatively inexpensive stamps of Sardinia that an Italian dealer once discovered a copy of a used 10c of the unissued series among a group of Sardinia 10c issues. He paid only a few cents for the gem.

Scott catalog lists no price for the unissued Neapolitan Provinces set. The Sassone specialized Italian stamp catalog does include prices for these stamps, and these prices reflect the extreme rarity of used copies.

A copy of the 10c on cover catalogs at 200 million lire (about $120,000); a used copy off cover is listed at 40 million lire (about $24,000). Used copies of the 30c and 80c are listed at 125 million lire ($90,000). Catalog prices for the other used values are: 5c, 35 million lire ($21,000); and 40c, 100 million lire ($60,000).

Unused copies are far easier to obtain. Sassone prices the mint stamps from $3 to $90.

ITALY

Neapolitan Nightmares

VALUE: $12,500
This ½-tornesi black error of color stamp was used only at Roccagloriosa in the Neapolitan Provinces.

The Neapolitan Provinces issued only eight stamps in its brief history, but several scarce errors occurred among these issues. The most expensive rarities among these are the ½-tornesi and 2-grana color errors.

Just prior to the unification of the Kingdom of Italy in 1862, the Kingdom of Naples and other provinces of southern Italy were united in the Neapolitan Provinces.

The newly formed provinces issued eight imperforate stamps in 1861 portraying King Victor Emmanuel II. The ½t was printed in green and the 2g in blue. However, both stamps were discovered printed in black, the color used for the 1g denomination.

According to L.N. and M. Williams' *Rare Stamps*, the ½t errors all bear the postmark of Roccagloriosa. The 2g was used at Potenza. Scott catalog lists the ½t black at $8,500 unused and $12,500 used; the 2g black catalogs at $18,500 used.

While the color errors are the scarcest of the Neapolitan Provinces issues, other errors in this series also bring high prices. Copies of the ½t and 5g are known printed on both sides. Unused examples are listed in Scott at $12,500 and $6,000, respectively.

Other varieties also have been discovered. The ½t, ½g, 1g, 2g, 5g and 20g denominations exist with the king's head upside down. Scott's prices for these range from $60 to $8,500. However, collectors should beware. Several forgeries of these inverted head errors have been created by applying a faked embossed head to printer's waste produced without the head.

In 1862 the Neapolitan Provinces joined the other Italian states in the Kingdom of Italy. Italy's stamps replaced the provincial issues. Though the Neapolitan Provinces issued stamps for less than a year, it provided collectors with some magnificent rarities.

Stamps Arrived; Flight Didn't

VALUE: $2,000

This Liberian rarity was produced for a Pan American flight between Liberia and the United States which eventually was postponed.

A postponed flight resulted in two of Liberia's most interesting stamps. In the 1930's, Liberia's mail destined for the United States went by boat or was flown to Europe to connect with flights bound for the United States. Either way, the mail took several weeks, and sometimes months, to reach its destination.

So Liberians were excited when Pan American Airways announced that it would provide direct airmail service between Liberia and the United States. This African nation was founded in 1822 by U.S. black freedmen, and many of their descendants still had close ties in the United States.

Pan Am announced its plans for the service in early September 1941; the inaugural flight was to take place September 29. This hardly allowed time for special airmail stamps to be printed to commemorate the flight, so the Liberian Post Office overprinted its 1938 set of ten airmails "First Flight/LIBERIA—U.S./1941."

All but two of the values (50¢ brown and $1 blue) were surcharged with a 50¢ denomination. A single bar obliterated the eight original values.

Collectors prepared covers for the first flight, affixing the specially overprinted stamps. These issues were available in New York City at the Liberian Consulate, as well as in Monrovia.

At the last minute, Pan Am postponed the flight. Wartime restrictions and other problems made it impossible for the airmail service to take place. The Liberian Post Office was left holding bags of covers. Its officials made the only logical decision. The covers were sent to their destinations by former, established airmail routes.

The surcharged stamps catalog from $30 to $2,750. The 50¢ on 1¢ green and 50¢ on 20¢ magenta are the scarcest in unused condition, cataloging at $2,750 and $2,000 respectively.

A single of the 50¢ on 20¢ was part of the Josiah K. Lilly collection auctioned by Robert A. Siegel in 1967.

Pan Am rescheduled the flight in 1942, and the 1941 overprinted stamps were reissued, this time with two bars obliterating the "1941." But these rescheduled flight stamps are common, cataloging between $3.50 and $8 each.

The "Second-Fiddle" Rarities

VALUE: $40,000
This early impression example of a 2d was owned by Josiah Lilly.

VALUE: $32,500
Reengraved Post Paid 2-penny stamps are known as Fillet Heads.

The famous Post Office Mauritius stamps of 1847 overshadow their successors, the Post Paid Mauritius stamps. When placed against the $400,000 and $250,000 Scott catalog values of the Post Office issues, the $525 to $60,000 prices for the Post Paid stamps seem comparatively pale.

It is hard to believe that a $60,000 stamp can be considered second-rate, but the Post Paid issues have taken a backseat. Every book about rare stamps touts the Post Office Mauritius issue, but the Post Paid stamps seldom are mentioned.

Nevertheless, the Post Paid Mauritius issues are among the world's greatest rarities and deserve at least some of the limelight.

That the Post Office stamps are scarcer cannot be subject to argument. Only 500 of each value were issued. And the story linked to them is more romantic. Every collector visualizes the nearly blind watchmaker, Joseph Barnard, sitting in his dark shop in Port Louis engraving the first stamps of the British colony. He mistook the words "Post Paid" for "Post Office" and mistakenly engraved the latter on the stamps.

The error quickly was caught, accounting for the scarcity of these stamps today. New stamps were issued in 1848 carrying the appropriate "Post Paid" inscription. These also were printed locally in Port Louis in values of 1-penny and 2d.

Although not as scarce as their predecessors, the Post Paid issues are rare. The same plates were used again and again for these issues, and the lines in the background became so worn that they eventually disappeared. The stamps, therefore, are classified as to earliest, early, intermediate, and worn impressions.

The first or earliest impression is the scarcest. The 1d catalogs in Scott at $37,500 mint and $22,500 used. The 2d is listed at $40,000 mint and $22,500 used. Later impressions range in catalog value from $525 to $18,000.

VALUE: $60,000

The "PENOE" engraver's error occurred in the seventh position of the second printing plate.

Once again, however, the engraver erred. He engraved "PENOE" instead of "PENCE" in the seventh position on the second plate. The earliest impression of this error catalogs at $60,000 mint and $30,000 used — definitely rarities in anyone's book.

King George V purchased a block of five with the "PENOE" error for the Royal Collection. Josiah Lilly owned an early impression of the normal 2d and an intermediate impression of the "PENOE" error. These were auctioned by Robert A. Siegel in 1967.

A beautiful folded letter franked with both the 1d and 2d stamps, intermediate impressions, was auctioned in the Siegel Rarities of the World sale April 20, 1985. It realized $32,500

This letter is addressed to Port Louis. The stamps are tied by "3" in target cancellations. The letter also features a framed "Souillac De 18 1855" postmark and a crown "Mauritius GPO Dec 19 1855" postmark. It once was part of the Maurice Burrus collection.

In 1859 an engraver, Sherwin, reengraved the badly worn plates that were used for the Post Paid Mauritius stamps. Only the 2d reengraved stamps were placed in circulation. The 1d plate was reengraved but never used. The 2d stamps are known as the Fillet Head issue. They are priced in the Scott catalog at $32,500 mint and $5,000 used.

Collectors should beware. Sheets of the Fillet Heads were produced in 1877 by an autotype process from the original plates by the Autotype Company in England. Occasionally, these copies of the 2d have been sold as genuine stamps.

The autotype sheets did serve a useful purpose. They helped collectors locate plate positions of the genuine issue.

Mexico's District Hidalgos

VALUE: $22,500 plus

Only one cover bearing the 1-peso district of Monterrey overprint rarity has been authenticated as genuine. It is postmarked July 24, 1864.

Mexico's 1864 Hidalgo stamps, overprinted for the districts of Monterrey or Saltillo, have gained the attention of both collectors and counterfeiters for many years.

Mexico was divided into 56 districts in 1856. That same year, the Mexican Post Office provided the main post offices in each district with a handstamp bearing the district name. Postmasters were instructed to overprint stamp supplies with their district names.

Stamps of some districts are scarcer than others. The 1864 "SALTILLO" and "MONTERREY" overprints are among the scarcest. The 1-real, 2r, 4r and 1-peso stamps were printed by the American Bank Note Company on yellowish paper.

War had plagued Mexico for many years. Then, the French invaded the country in 1863. Chaos was everywhere. The Mexican government retreated first to Saltillo, then to Monterrey. Few of the "SALTILLO" and "MONTERREY" overprinted stamps were ever used. For this reason, used overprinted stamps are much harder to find than unused copies.

The rarest is the 1p in used condition. Scott lists used copies of this denomination at $22,500. Only one cover bearing the 1p has been authenticated. It was mailed from Monterrey to Fresnillo July 24, 1864. This rarity was part of the impressive Mexico collection formed by John M. Taylor.

When Irwin Heiman sold the Taylor collection in 1960, a New Jersey collector bought the cover. Heiman again sold the cover in 1975 to a Mexican specialist who wishes to remain anonymous.

Stamps from this series without the district overprints are from remainder stocks. Only those with the overprints are considered to have been genuinely issued.

However, these cheaper stamps without the overprints have provided counterfeiters with an opportunity to create forged overprints and cancellations. Collectors should have used overprinted stamps of this series expertized. The 1r exists with a "1/2" surcharge in black, but this is a bogus marking.

In 1867 the Hidalgo stamps were reprinted on white paper but never officially issued. "NATIONAL BANK NOTE COMPANY" appears in the sheet margins of these reprints.

The Invisible Rarity

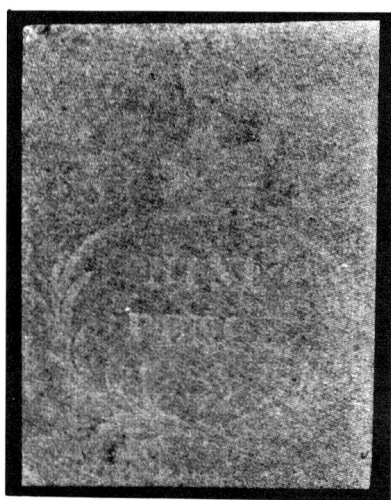 

VALUE: $75,000

The embossed design is barely visible on this Natal 9-penny rarity (left). The illustration at right shows what was embossed on the "invisible" design.

Few collectors have seen, much less owned, a copy of one of Natal's first issues. The crudely embossed stamps resemble colored blotting paper. The designs can only be detected upon close examination. Yet, a copy of the 9-penny blue of this set realized $75,000 at auction in 1984.

Issued in 1857, the stamps are actually provisionals. The government of Natal introduced the set to indicate prepayment of postage until the intended first issue arrived from England. Natal was a primitive country. Native runners still carried the mail from the port of Durban to the capital of Pietermaritzburg.

The regular stamps were being printed in England and were to arrive in 1860. The government needed stamps immediately. Therefore, it commissioned F. Davis and Sons, a printer in Pietermaritzburg, to print four values.

The printer knew nothing about producing postage stamps. The only paper sheets he had on hand were similar to blotting paper, but he had them in several colors.

Davis used the resources he had available. He engraved separate dies for each denomination. The stamps show a crown, the initials "VR" (Victoria Regina) and the denomination. Four different embossed shapes were used. Davis printed the stamps one at a time. The denominations and colors were 3d rose, 6d green, 9d blue and 1-shilling buff.

The scarcity of these issues is due in part to the way they were printed. They were imperforate, and the colorless embossing made it difficult to see the designs. Because of this, many of the stamps were destroyed by improper cutting. Cut squares are rare. Also, the towns of Durban and Pietermaritzburg were sparsely populated. Few people wrote letters, so few stamps were printed.

Collectors today must search long and hard for copies of these issues. When they find them, they must pay high prices to add them to their albums.

The 3d is the least expensive, cataloging in Scott at $600 used. The other values catalog at $1,200 for the 6d green, $7,500 for the 9d blue, and $4,500 for the 1/- buff. All prices are for used condition. The only mint example is the 9d blue. It was sold for $75,000 at the March 29, 1984 auction conducted by the Colonial Stamp Company of Los Angeles.

The embossed design on this stamp, as with the other values, is barely visible. Yet, a collector was willing to pay $75,000 for a crudely printed stamp from this little known British colony.

In 1858 Natal introduced a 1d denomination. Again, the printer used colorless embossing. The design features a crown with the country name below. However, the value was produced in three different colors — blue, rose and buff. Catalog prices range from $900 for the blue and buff to $1,000 for the rose.

Sydney Views: Head to Toe

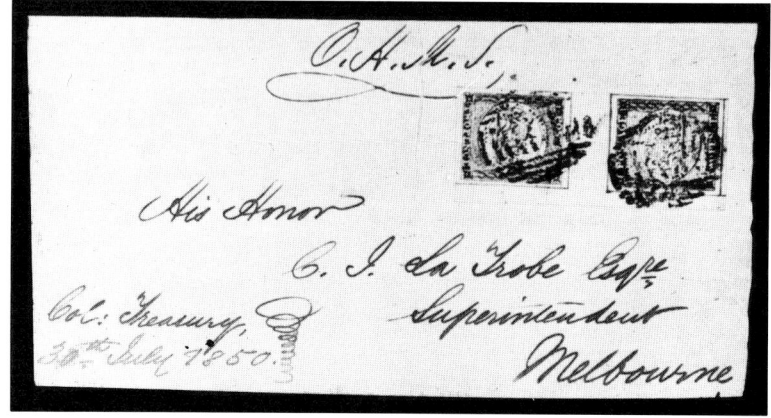

VALUE: $5,500 plus

A tete-beche pair of the New South Wales 2-penny Sydney Views stamps frank this cover — a one-of-a-kind item currently worth over $5,500.

The Anne Boyd Lichtenstein Foundation owns a spectacular cover franked with a tete-beche pair of the 1850 New South Wales 2-penny Sydney Views stamp. The cover is the only one of its kind. It was discovered in 1903 by an Australian collector.

Alfred F. Lichtenstein, the famous collector from New York, later bought it. He bequeathed it to his daughter, Louise Boyd Dale. Upon her death, the Anne Boyd Lichtenstein Foundation became the owner of the cover.

New South Wales, now part of the Commonwealth of Australia, issued its first stamps in 1850. The designs, by Robert Clayton of Sydney, are based on the great seal of the colony featuring a view of Sydney with a symbolic figure of Industry seated on a bale of merchandise. She is pictured releasing convicts and pointing to oxen plowing. Collectors dubbed the series "Sydney Views."

The tete-beche pair is the scarcest of all the Sydney Views

stamps. (Tete-beche means stamps which are printed next to each other with one design inverted to the normal stamp.)

Most tete-beche pairs are created when a cliche is inserted upside down in the printing plate. However, such is not the case with the 2d Sydney Views tete-beche pair.

In Volume 4 of his *Encyclopaedia of British Empire Postage Stamps*, Robson Lowe explains that sheets larger than the size necessary were used to produce the pane of 24 2d stamps. So, a portion of the sheet was printed; then the sheet was turned around to print the remaining portion. The result is known as a print-and-turn tete-beche pair.

The Sydney Views are expensive stamps, with Scott catalog values ranging from $250 to $5,500. What this cover bearing the only known tete-beche pair of this issue would bring if it were ever put up for sale or auction is pure speculation.

Chalon Heads of the 1850's

VALUE: $20,000
Andre Chalon's full-face portrait of Britain's Queen Victoria appears on New Zealand's first stamps.

Andre Chalon's coronation portrait of Queen Victoria appears on many classic issues of the British colonies, but among the most famous occurs on the first stamps of New Zealand. These classics are known as the "Chalon Heads" or "full-face Queens." The portrait by Chalon, a Swiss artist, shows the queen in full robes of state, although the stamps reproduce only the portrait's bust.

The New Zealand government decided to issue stamps in 1854 and commissioned Perkins Bacon & Company in London to print them. The rarest of the first three denominations is this 1-penny dull carmine. This stamp covered the rate for soldiers' letters. It was printed on white paper. The other two values, 2d deep blue and 1-shilling yellow green, appear on blued paper. Although not as rare as the 1d, these values are scarce, nonetheless.

Scott prices this set (unused and used) as follows: 1d, $20,000, $10,000; 2d, $9,500, $850; and 1/-, $15,000, $4,250.

Perkins Bacon shipped some imperforate stamps to New Zealand along with a press, the plates, ink and a supply of the large star watermarked paper used for this issue. The set made its debut July 18, 1855. Perkins Bacon had produced only a small quantity of stamps (12,000 1d, 66,000 2d and 8,000 1/-), and this inadequate supply soon was exhausted.

Since Perkins Bacon had supplied the necessary equipment to produce more stamps, the New Zealand government hired John Richardson of Auckland to print another issue. However, Richardson did not use the large star watermarked paper sent by the British printer. He used an unwatermarked blue paper instead.

The same denominations were produced, but the colors are much brighter — 1d orange-red, 2d blue and 1/- green. Once again, the stamps are imperf. This second issue also is expensive, cataloging in Scott (unused and used) at: 1d, $4,500, $1,200; 2d, $2,750, $450; and 1/-, $15,000, $2,750.

In 1857 the New Zealand Post Office authorized a 6d postal rate on ½-ounce letters to Great Britain. However, no 6d stamps existed for this purpose. Therefore, the post office authorized the bisecting (or cutting in half) of the 1/- denominations of both the London and Auckland printing for this purpose. These bisects are also among the greatest rarities of these issues, cataloging in Scott at $20,000 for the London printing and $15,000 for the Auckland printing.

The paper used by Richardson carried the name of its producer, "Sands & McDougall, Melbourne," and a few of the stamps bear part of the lettering from this inscription.

Richardson produced another issue of stamps from 1858 to 1861, this time adding the 6d brown denomination to the other three. These are found on thin hard or thick soft white paper.

Experimental perforations began appearing on New Zealand's stamps in 1859, including pin rouletted, serrate rouletted, rouletted, and perf 13. Although some of these perf varieties are expensive, prices decline for the later issues of New Zealand so that they are within reach of most collectors.

A few rarities still exist among these later issues, including the 3d brown lilac on pelure paper. While all values on this pelure paper, used in 1862, are scarce, the 3d is the scarcest because it never was placed into use. The Chalon Heads remained in use until 1872, when a profile portrait of Queen Victoria facing left replaced the full-face portrait designed by Chalon.

Overprinted "Oil Rivers"

VALUE: $150,000

This 20-shilling surcharge on a 1-shilling stamp of Great Britain, overprinted for use in Oil Rivers, is the scarcest of Oil Rivers provisionals.

    The Niger Coast Protectorate probably has the distinction of producing the greatest number of philatelic rarities within the shortest time. Its Oil Rivers provisionals are among the world's most valuable stamps, with prices reaching $100,000 or more for a few.

    In the late 1800's, the territory known as the Oil Rivers Protectorate (later renamed Niger Coast Protectorate) was administered by the Royal Niger Company. At first, the Royal Niger Company handstamped letters with its insignia. However, in 1892, the British government appointed Sir Claude Maxwell MacDonald as commissioner of the territory, and Sir Claude brought with him a supply of overprinted stamps from England.

    The stamps were Britain's 1881-87 issues with the inscription "BRITISH/PROTECTORATE/OIL RIVERS" overprinted in black. Thomas De La Rue of England applied the overprints.

    Only one of these provisionals can be considered rare. The overprint was applied too low on the sheet resulting in the wording "OIL RIVERS" appearing above "BRITISH/PROTECTORATE." Scott catalog lists this error at $7,000 unused or used.

In September 1893, provisionals were produced locally by surcharging the already overprinted 1-penny lilac stamps of Great Britain. The surcharge consisted of "½d" values on both sides of a diagonal line which extended from the upper right corner to the lower left. Thus, two ½d stamps were created from one. The user cut along the diagonal line, making two bisected stamps.

The printers used a violet surcharge on these stamps at first, but they found that the violet was nearly invisible on the lilac stamps. Only 480 1d stamps received the violet surcharge; the printers then changed to red ink. Scott catalog lists the violet surcharged issues at $6,500 unused, while those with the red catalog at $200 unused or used. A double overprint on the stamp with the violet surcharge is the gem of this issue. It catalogs at $13,000.

Another shortage of ½d stamps occurred in December 1893, and the postal officials authorized the surcharging of the remaining values of stamps brought by Sir Claude. The 2d and 2½d values surcharged with the new ½d denomination met a specific need, augmenting the nearly depleted supplies of ½d stamps.

However, a few high values also were created by surcharging the 2d, 5d and 1/- stamps. No apparent need for these denominations existed, and they possibly were produced for philatelic reasons. Oddly, these are the great rarities of this series. Only 28 copies of the 5/- violet surcharge on 2d green and carmine exist, including one with an inverted surcharge.

Those with the normal surcharges catalog at $16,500 unused and used; the invert is not listed, but probably would bring a much higher price. Thirty-two copies of the 10/- on 5d exist, including one invert. Again, these stamps catalog at $16,500 unused and used.

Three colors of surcharges were applied to the 1/- green to create 20/- stamps. Only five of the violet surcharge exist, including one invert, plus only two or three of the red surcharge.

Two copies of the black surcharge are known, although the status of one has been questioned. C.J. Lucas owned one copy; it was sent to him on a letter by Sir Claude. The stamp now is in the Royal Collection at Buckingham Palace in London. Count Phillippe von Ferrari owned the second copy; however, some collectors dispute its authenticity, saying the stamp is a proof or forgery.

The violet surcharges catalog at $100,000, while the red and black list at $150,000. These stamps exist only unused.

In late 1893, the provisional issues of Oil Rivers were replaced by regular stamps portraying Queen Victoria. The "Oil Rivers" inscription soon was dropped from the stamps because the territory was renamed Niger Coast Protectorate. This, however, was not to mark the end to the provisionals.

In 1894 the territory experienced a shortage of ½d and 1d stamps. A ½d red surcharge was overprinted on the 1893 Niger Coast 1d light blue. These surcharged issues catalog in Scott at $1,000 unused and $240 used, with an inverted surcharge listed at $5,000. The 1d vermilion Niger Coast stamps were similarly surcharged in black, violet and blue. Catalog prices for these issues range from $300 to $1,500.

A 1d stamp was created by surcharging the Oil Rivers 2d green and carmine provisional. A double surcharge error exists and catalogs at $1,650 unused and $1,500 used; an inverted surcharge is listed at $1,500 used. As with the earlier bisects, these ½d and 1d surcharges were applied to halves of the stamps creating bisects.

The final provisional for Niger Coast Protectorate made its debut later in 1894. It is a "ONE/HALF PENNY" black surcharge applied to the Niger Coast 2½d blue. A double surcharge on this issue catalogs at $2,000 unused and $1,800 used.

Another error occurs in the surcharge inscription. It reads "OIE" instead of "ONE." Scott lists it at $1,700 unused and $1,600 used. This error is compounded by a double surcharge variety, which catalogs at $3,250.

In 1900 the Niger Coast Protectorate was incorporated into Southern Nigeria, and the stamps of Southern Nigeria replaced those of the protectorate. But in the short time the protectorate had issued its own stamps, it provided stamp collectors with a rather confusing host of philatelic gems.

Too High To Buy

VALUE: $45,000

Northern Nigeria's 1904 25-pound stamp is that country's great rarity.

Northern Nigeria's 1904 £25 stamp is not only an unusually high value, it is also that country's greatest rarity. The stamp made its debut in April 1904. Like the other issues of this west African country, it is inscribed "POSTAGE & REVENUE," meaning it could be used for postal or fiscal purposes. However, the £25 stamp was intended almost solely for fiscal use.

The stamp featured the common design used by many of the British colonies at that time, showing a portrait of King Edward VII. Collectors refer to these issues as "key plates" because the common portion — the portrait, frame and "Postage & Revenue" inscription — was on one plate. A second plate was employed for the parts of the design that changed — the value tablet and name of the colony. Some of the other countries using this particular common, or "key plate" design, were Straits Settlements, Cayman Islands, Ceylon and Fiji.

Key plate printing was an economical method of printing because it limited the number of plates needed for the colonies. The key plate could be used for several different countries.

This high-value Northern Nigeria stamp shocked and angered collectors when it made its debut. They shied away from buying this issue because it was too expensive. They viewed its value as unnecessary. However, collectors were unaware that this stamp would become even more expensive in a short time.

Soon after the £25 was issued, postal authorities also realized there was little need for this denomination. The collectors refused to buy it, it was unnecessary postally, and even as a fiscal, there was little demand for the stamp. So, this issue was withdrawn shortly after it was introduced.

Collectors soon found that the £25 face value was cheap compared to the prices the stamp brought after it was withdrawn from sale. It was no longer available, very few had been sold, and collectors paid dearly for a copy. No used copies exist today. Scott catalog lists unused copies at $45,000.

In just a few days, the Northern Nigeria £25 earned not only the title of the country's highest denominated stamp and its most controversial issue, but also the designation as its greatest rarity.

NOVA SCOTIA

When Duller Was Brighter

VALUE: $110,000

The exotic city of Madras, destination of this cover, adds appeal to this mourning envelope with its two Nova Scotia 1-shilling dull violet stamps.

Nova Scotia's 1851 1-shilling stamps rank among the philatelic gems of the British Commonwealth. This British colony issued its own stamps for only a short time. Stamps of Nova Scotia were replaced by those of Canada in 1867.

But in the short period from 1851 until its union with Canada, Nova Scotia issued stamps which include some of the world's great rarities. The 1/- stamps are part of Nova Scotia's first series introduced in 1851. This denomination was issued in two shades of violet. Scott catalog describes these as reddish violet and dull violet. Stanley Gibbons catalog lists them as purple and cold violet.

Only a small number (5,120) of the dull violet (cold violet) 1/- stamps were sent to the colony, thus accounting for their scarcity. The dull violet is an intense, almost metallic shade, and the stamp is one of the most beautiful in the world. Only a dozen unused copies are known today.

The reddish violet (purple) was from the second printing of this denomination. Although it carries an expensive price tag, it is not nearly as scarce as its dull violet counterpart. The printing total was 49,920 stamps. No unused multiples of either are known.

The 1/- denomination was used to pay multiple rates on letters, but the only properly used 1/- dull violet stamps appear on correspondence to India. This correspondence is particularly interesting to stamp and postal history collectors. The covers are addressed to Walter Lawrence Ingles in Madras, India.

Just the mention of the city of Madras brings thoughts of mystery and exotic marketplaces to mind, so it is no wonder that this correspondence has enticed collectors over the years. The most famous of these Madras items is a mourning cover with a pair of the 1/- dull violet and a single of the 1851 6-penny stamp of Nova Scotia.

This mourning cover was part of the Alfred Lichtenstein collection which he bequeathed to his daughter, Louise Boyd Dale. It realized $20,000 during the Dale-Lichtenstein collection auction conducted by H.R. Harmer in 1969. In the same sale, a folded cover bearing two singles of the 1/- reddish violet with a 3d and 6d was purchased for $22,000.

The mourning cover was auctioned once again in October 1984 by Christie's/Robson Lowe in New York City. Although it failed to reach its estimate of $125,000, it did realize an astounding $110,000.

PUERTO RICO

The Mayor's Stamp

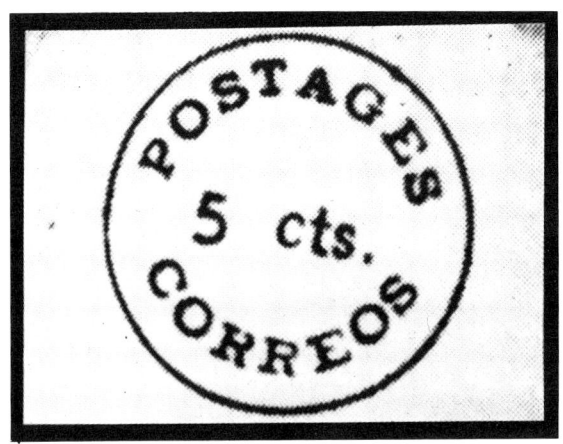

VALUE: $6,000

The Ponce provisional stamp was born after an invasion of Puerto Rico by United States forces in 1898.

During the Spanish American War, United States troops invaded Puerto Rico, encountering little resistance from the islanders. A provisional handstamp issued on the island following this invasion has become Puerto Rico's rarest stamp. Scott catalog prices it at $6,000 in mint condition.

The first military postal service in Puerto Rico opened at Ponce August 3, 1898, at the request of Ponce's mayor, R.U. Colom. Colom had written to General Wilson, who was acting military governor of the conquered island, to get U.S. approval for such a postal service.

Having received permission from General Wilson, Colom started the postal service, and a special handstamped provisional was released to indicate prepayment of mail. The crudely produced handstamp consisted of the words "POSTAGES CORREOS" within a circle, with "5 cts." in the center. The provisional was applied in violet ink to yellowish white gummed paper, which was then cut out and affixed to envelopes.

Later, the military post office began impressing the Ponce coat of arms in violet or black over the stamp as a control mark to make counterfeiting more difficult. Nevertheless, many counterfeits of this issue exist today.

The provisional stamp was used for only a short time. It has become one of the scarcest of all U.S. possessions stamps. In the United States Possessions Philatelic Society journal, *Possessions*, published in the third quarter 1981, Gilbert N. Pass notes that only 17 different copies of the Ponce item have been recorded.

In addition to the cutout adhesive copies, the provisional exists applied directly to envelopes and used along with regular stamps. The handstamp also has been imprinted on U.S. stamps. These imprinted stamps probably were made to order.

Printed Too Soon

VALUE: $16,500

The tiny island of Reunion is responsible for two of the world's great rarities.

Some of the world's great philatelic rarities have come from small stamp issuing entities which are little known to collectors. One such entity is Reunion. This island in the Indian Ocean is smaller in land area than Rhode Island.

Stamp collectors hardly would expect rarities from this former French colony, which is best known for its "CFA" overprints on French stamps. However, Reunion's first stamps catalog in Scott at $16,500 unused and $9,000 used. Such great collectors as Alfred Caspary and Thomas Tapling sought and acquired examples of these rare stamps.

Reunion issued its first stamps in 1852, just 12 years after the introduction of the first adhesive stamp, Great Britain's Penny Black, and three years after France released its first issue.

Unlike either of those stamps, Reunion's first set showed no portrait; instead they featured two different ornamental designs. Produced locally in Reunion's capital of St. Denis by Lahuppe, they were printed by letterpress, imperforate, and without gum. The denominations were 15 centimes and 30c.

But the people on Reunion were not ready for stamps. Few were ever used. Most of the sheets of stamps remained at the post office until they were ordered destroyed in 1860.

This issue was reprinted several times, and collectors are cautioned that these reprints are cheap. Scott lists them at $12 each. They are easily identified. The reprints are printed on a more bluish, unglazed paper and are framed by a single outer line and thin inner line. The originals have one thick and two thin lines.

Russia's First of Many

VALUE: $7,250 plus
Less than a half dozen copies of the
Russian Tiflis local stamp exist.

Many collectors believe the first postage stamp of Russia was issued in 1858 by the Imperial Government. However, a 6-kopeck stamp was used in the Georgian capital of Tiflis four months earlier.

Rumors circulated in the late 1880's about the existence of such a stamp, but no copies had come to light. So, in 1889, Jean-Baptiste Moens, a stamp dealer in Brussels, Belgium, wrote to the postmaster in Tiflis requesting information on the stamp. The postmaster confirmed that such an issue was in use in late 1857 and early 1858, but said that no copies had been discovered.

The first photograph of the Tiflis local stamp was not published until 1924 when K.K. Schmidt, a specialist in Russian stamps, described this issue in a magazine on Russian philately. Schmidt exhibited this rarity for the first time in 1930 at the IPOSTA philatelic exhibition in Berlin.

It seems that the postmaster in Tiflis, the Georgian capital located in the Caucasus, jumped the gun and introduced a stamp prior to the release of the imperial issues. He issued the local stamp at the request of his viceroy.

The stamp was printed in colorless embossing and featured the Tiflis coat of arms and the double-headed eagle, the symbol of the czar. The inscription, in Russian, reads "Town Post of Tiflis 6 kop." The stamp is imperforate but gummed. It is a small stamp, measuring only 22 millimeters square.

This issue owes its scarcity to the fact that it was in use for only four months; it was withdrawn as soon as the imperial stamps were introduced in March 1858. Also, if they wanted to affix their own stamps, the general public could only purchase the Tiflis local in strips of five. Since they could go to the post office and have the clerk affix the appropriate amount of postage to their letters, there was little reason to buy an entire strip of five.

Less than a half dozen copies of this stamp exist. Agathon Faberge, the famous Russian collector and jeweler who also owned several rare Russian zemstvo stamps, acquired three examples of the Tiflis local. All three were auctioned during the 1939 H.R. Harmer sale of the Faberge collection.

Robert A. Siegel sold a copy in 1971, formerly in the Stibbe collection, for $7,250. Location of the Schmidt copy is unknown.

Spain's Other Color Error

VALUE: $15,000 plus

Arthur Hind, noted collector of worldwide stamps, owned a block of 12 of this 5-real red brown error.

Many collectors are familiar with the story of Spain's 2-real blue error of color. Collectors argued for years over whether the stamp was a true error of color or a proof. They finally agreed it was a genuine error.

This famous stamp has overshadowed another error of color — Spain's 1851 5r red brown. This 5r error stamp also puzzled collectors for many years.

Unlike the more famous 2r blue, which resulted from a cliche of the 2r being inserted in the plate of the 6r blue, the 5r red brown was more difficult to explain. No other stamp in this series was printed in red brown. The normal 1851 5r issue was printed in rose.

Some collectors believed the stamp to be a trial printing, which somehow found its way into the hands of collectors. However, a letter was discovered from Senor Zaragoza, who was director general of posts in Spain when the 1851 5r stamp was issued. Zaragoza's letter offers an explanation.

He says that it had been called to his attention that a shipment of the 5r sent to the Canary Islands was the wrong shade of red (red brown instead of rose). In his letter, he ordered the stamps withdrawn and replaced with stamps in the normal color.

The Spanish Post Office was able to recover most of the red brown stamps and destroy them. Of course, in doing so, they created another gem for philately.

Scott catalog lists the 5r red brown error of color at $15,000 mint and $7,500 used.

Which Value Is Correct?

VALUE: $5,000

The numeral of value on this Swedish stamp says "20," but the value inscription "tretio" means 30 ore.

A careless workman and a negligent inspector were responsible for the release of one of Sweden's most famous errors to its mailing public. The stamp, known as the Tretio error, today catalogs at $5,000 unused and $4,000 used in the Scott *Standard Postage Stamp Catalogue*.

The Swedish Post Office used two designs for its stamps issued from 1872 to 1879. One featured the denomination expressed as a numeral in the center with "FRIMARKE" at the top of the surrounding circle and the value spelled out below. The other design showed the coat of arms in the center with the inscriptions in the surrounding circle similar to the first design.

In 1879 the Swedish Post Office ordered a new printing of these issues. However, the superintendent of the printing office noticed that one of the subjects on the plate of 20-ore stamps was damaged. To save time and money, he ordered one of the workers to drill out the figure "30" and word "TRETIO" from one of the 30o subjects and replace it with "20" and "TJUGO."

The workman replaced the numeral, but he forgot to replace the wording. Thus, the creation of one of Sweden's greatest errors — a 20o stamp with the wording "TRETIO" from the 30o value.

The superintendent approved the plate, failing to notice the error. Of the 6,000 sheets printed, 182 were destroyed, not because of the error, but because they did not measure up to other standards in the inspection. Nearly 1,600 sheets were distributed to the post offices in Sweden before postal officials detected the error. The officials ordered the immediate withdrawal of these sheets, but only 613 were recovered.

Another 4,235 of the errors were discovered in the stock at the Swedish Post Office. On March 31, 1880, the post office burned the 4,848 copies it had recovered.

More than 50 examples of the Tretio error exist, with the most recent discovery being an imperforate on an envelope addressed to a Lloyd's of London underwriter. The Swedish Postal Museum in Stockholm owns one of the most striking examples of this error. It is in a pair se-tenant with a normal 20o.

Forgeries exist of the Tretio error, including those produced by famed Swiss forger Francois Fournier.

The "In-between" Issue

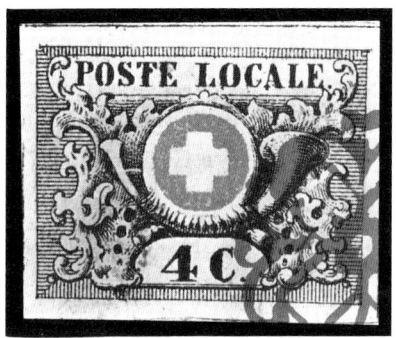

VALUE: $16,000

The 4-centime transitional stamp of Geneva is truly rare, but it has failed to achieve its deserved recognition.

Stamp collectors the world over associate the Swiss canton of Geneva with the famous Double Geneva stamps. Another Geneva rarity, however, has failed to gain the recognition it deserves. This neglected issue is the 4-centime transitional stamp of 1849.

The cantonals of Zurich, Basel and Geneva issued their own stamps prior to the formation of the Swiss Federation in 1848. However, Switzerland adopted a constitution that year establishing federal power over the cantons making up the Swiss Confederation.

Stamps for the federal administration were not introduced until 1850, but two cantons — Zurich and Geneva — issued transitional stamps to recognize the new status of the nation. Zurich replaced its numeral designs with the federation's coat of arms; Geneva likewise replaced its own arms designs with the federation arms.

While the 2½-rappen issue of Zurich and the two 5c stamps of Geneva are expensive, the 4c of Geneva is extremely scarce. Collector Alfred Caspary managed to obtain two covers bearing singles of the 4c and a piece with a horizontal pair. The used pair later was purchased by Maurice Burrus. Scott catalog lists the 4c at $27,500 unused and $16,000 used.

Upsetting the King

VALUE: $4,620
Tonga's first pictorial series included a rarity — an inverted center on the 7½-penny King George II stamp.

The South Pacific island group of Tonga began issuing stamps in 1886. The designs consisted of crude portraits of the king or its coat of arms — not much to capture the collector's eye.

In 1897 Tonga introduced its first pictorial issue, a beautiful set of stamps featuring scenes of the islands, flora and fauna, and a favorable portrait of the islands' King George II.

A Mr. Lieber, who lived on the islands, purchased a sheet of the 7½-penny pictorial stamps, portraying the king, at his local post office in 1900. Upon returning home, he discovered, much to his delight, that the monarch's head was upside down on each of the 60 stamps in the sheet. He had purchased a major error!

Prior to the production of this issue, Tongan stamps were printed and surcharged in New Zealand. Few errors had occurred, with the exception of the normal varieties in the surcharges which can be expected. It is true that a horizontal pair of the 1895 King George II

1d stamp was discovered imperforate between — an exceptional rarity. But for the most part, Tonga's early issues provided little excitement for the collector.

The spectacular 7½d inverted center made collectors take notice of the stamps of the islands, which had been dubbed the "Friendly Isles" by Captain James Cook.

When the Tongan Post Office began planning the pictorial series, it decided to pull out all the stops and to hire the highly esteemed Thomas De La Rue firm in England to print its new stamps.

De La Rue to this day is known for its impeccable printing quality. However, an occasional error does slip by the printer's inspectors. This time it was an entire sheet of inverted centers.

De La Rue printed the bicolored 7½d in two separate processes — one for the green frame and one for the black portrait. One sheet of stamps was turned upside down when it passed through the press the second time, resulting in the inverted centers.

These errors are priced in Scott catalog at $5,250 mint. Colonial Stamp Company of Los Angeles sold a copy at its June 1983 auction for $4,620, including a 10 percent buyer's commission.

UNITED STATES

First Dealer's Find

VALUE: $32,000

This New Haven postmaster's provisional entire has been in the collections of Sterling, Ferrari and Hind. Sterling first bought it for a mere 10¢.

In 1871 William P. Brown, reputedly the first stamp dealer in the United States, was examining a collection he had purchased when he came upon a cut square of the rare New Haven, Connecticut, postmaster's provisional.

Brown had never seen a stamp like this. One of the covers in the collection carried the name of a prominent lawyer in New Haven, so Brown contacted the lawyer for more information about the stamp.

He was shocked to learn that the collection had been stolen from the lawyer. Brown returned the collection to him along with the New Haven provisional. The lawyer was so grateful for the return of his collection that he gave Brown the provisional.

Since that time, only nine copies of the New Haven provisional have been discovered — six entires and three cut squares.

New Haven's Postmaster Edward A. Mitchell first conceived the idea of issuing a provisional stamp for his city to indicate the prepayment of postage. He commissioned Augustus E. Lines to prepare the original engraving and F.P. Gorham to make the brass handstamp. The stamp is very simple, carrying the inscription "POST OFFICE/NEW HAVEN, CT/5/PAID." It was issued in 1845.

Customers took their envelopes to the post office in New Haven (or they could buy envelopes from the postmaster). The envelopes were stamped with the provisional in red or blue ink. Mitchell then signed each envelope in red, blue or black ink to prevent forgeries.

Mitchell once stated that he believed no more than 2,000 copies of the provisional had been produced, accounting for its rarity today. Two of the existing copies of the provisional were from the Silliman collection. An envelope addressed to Francis Markoe Jr., Washington City, was sent by Benjamin Silliman Sr.

Edward Sterling, a New Jersey dealer, once bought this entire for 10¢. It later was in the collections of Count Phillippe Ferrari and Arthur Hind. A cut to shape copy in dull blue was discovered inside another letter written by Benjamin Silliman Jr. Harold C. Brooks found this copy in 1924 while going through envelopes which had been stored in an attic for 79 years.

In 1871 Mitchell's chief clerk, Cyrus Berry Peets, produced reprints of the New Haven provisional at Mitchell's request. These were printed in dull blue on white paper and signed by Mitchell. Each has the word "Copy" written on it.

Later, 30 reprints were produced, signed in red, dark blue and black. Reprints without the signature and on soft paper were created in 1890 for the infamous Nicholas F. Seebeck, known for his reprints of stamps of Central and South America.

The Mitchell family retained possession of the handstamp for several years. In 1923 Mitchell's grandson struck a few reprints using the date "1923" in place of the signature. The New Haven Philatelic Society purchased the handstamp and gave it to the New Haven Colony Historical Society.

Once again, reprints were created for a booklet which was sold for $5 to raise funds to defer the cost in purchasing the handstamp. The brass handstamp was partially defaced at that time in order to prevent further reprints.

The prices for the New Haven provisional in Scott's U.S. Specialized range from $2,000 for the cut to shape copy to $32,000 for the red provisional on light bluish paper with the signature in black. Scott gives no price for the dull blue on buff with signature in red.

UNITED STATES

Eleven 5's and One 10

VALUE: INDETERMINABLE

This cover, which bears two copies of the 5¢ Providence provisional, was owned by Alfred Caspary.

The Providence, Rhode Island, postmaster's provisional is best known for its unusual sheet arrangement. The sheet of 12 contained two stamp denominations — eleven 5¢ and one 10¢. The 10¢ was located in the upper right corner.

Providence Postmaster Welcome B. Sayles ordered the printing of these stamps in 1846 to serve as provisional issues until the United States Post Office Department issued stamps.

The provisionals were engraved on copper by George W. Babcock. They were printed on hard, yellowish-white homemade paper by Henry A. Hidden and Company in Providence. About 500 sheets were produced.

The stamps made their debut August 24, 1846. About 300 sheets had been sold when the provisionals were withdrawn from sale July 31, 1847, following the release of regular U.S. issues. The remaining 200 sheets were stored in the post office until 1850, when the post office was moved to a new location.

At that time, Sayles gave many of the sheets to one of his postmen, John Hagan. Hagan took them home and gave them to his children to play with. His wife even papered a wall in the attic with the stamps. When collectors began realizing the value of the stamps, Hagan's son, Fred, carefully removed them from the wall. Most of the stamps which exist today without gum were once affixed to the attic wall.

It also is said that Fred took some of the stamps to New York to be regummed. These have a yellowish, cracked gum compared to the almost white, smooth gum originally used on the stamps.

Used copies of the 5¢ provisional are scarce. Alfred Caspary, one of the great U.S. collectors, owned nine covers franked with the 5¢, including a fabulous cover featuring a pair. Caspary also owned a sheet of the provisionals, showing the unusual layout.

In his book, *Postmasters' Provisional Stamps*, John N. Luff states, ". . . only two 10¢ (both off cover) in this condition (used) have been reported." Hence, an uproar was created when a cover bearing a single of the 10¢ was submitted for an expertizing certificate.

VALUE: $12,500

This folded letter bearing a copy of the 10¢ Providence provisional stamp created a stir when it appeared. The cover was subjected to scientific testing, but was withdrawn from the Philatelic Foundation before it could be definitely authenticated.

The cover shows the stamp tied on a folded letter by a black manuscript checkmark and canceled by a red "PAID" marking, which was typical on used Providence provisionals. The stamp is barely tied by a red "10." This mark is typical on Providence provisional covers. The letter is from the same correspondence and year date as the cover in Caspary's collection franked with the pair of 5¢ stamps. It was sent to the same New Orleans destination.

But the expertizers were skeptical about the sudden appearance of this 10¢ cover. They subjected it to nondestructive laboratory analysis. They found that the ink of the red "PAID" postmark is of a different chemical content than the numeral and town postmarks on the cover. However, the tests showed that both inks were commonly used during this period.

The cover was withdrawn from the Philatelic Foundation prior to the reaching of an opinion, after over a year of examination by the expertizing committee. Because the committee did not reach a conclusion, Robert A. Siegel Auction Galleries sold the cover "as is" in its 1979 Rarities sale. It realized $12,500. Siegel's description said the cover was withdrawn from the foundation's expertizing service and sold "as is" because the owner wanted to finalize the sale. Only one other 10¢ cover is known; it is not tied.

The Scott U.S. Specialized lists the 10¢ on cover with pen cancel but gives no price. The mint single is priced at $950; se-tenant with the 5¢, $1,200; and the complete sheet, $3,850.

The 5¢ catalogs at $200 mint, $1,000 used. The cover with the 5¢ tied by postmark is listed at $12,000; the cover with pen cancel, $3,500. The cover franked with two 5¢ stamps is listed but not priced. A mint pair catalogs at $425, and a block of four at $950.

Reprints and counterfeits of the Providence provisionals also exist. Welcome Sayles gave the plate for the provisionals to his nephew, Lycurgus Sayles. His nephew then sold it to Bogert and Durbin Company. Bogert and Durbin cleaned the plate and used it to produce proofs on blue, green, red, brown and black cardboard.

Later, reprints were produced. Most of these bear one of the letters: "B.O.G.E.R.T.D.U.R.B.I.N." But some exist without the letters and can be troublesome to collectors. All Providence reprints are without gum. Some also were made by Livermore and Knight, who bought the plate from Bogert and Durbin. A.B. Slater later acquired the plate, giving it to the Rhode Island Historical Society.

UNITED STATES

The Frightening Ben Franklin

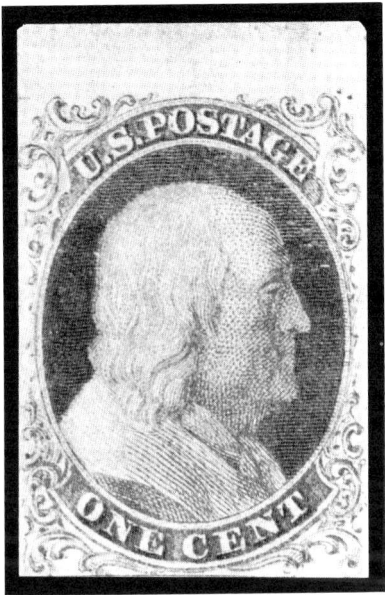

VALUE: $100,000

The 1851 1¢ blue type I is one of the great U.S. rarities and also one of the most studied stamps in the history of philately. The stamp comes from position 7 on the right pane of Plate I in its early printings.

A look at the 1851 1¢ blue Franklin issue of the United States in the Scott Specialized Catalogue of United States Stamps can be a frightening experience for collectors. Scott devotes a page and a half to the listing of the issue and its varieties.

A further look at the catalog values and the average collector may decide that these issues are beyond his price range. Indeed, the 1851 1¢ issue includes some of the greatest U.S. rarities.

The key to understanding this issue is to realize that the U.S. Post Office Department selected a design which proved to be too ornate for the printer, Toppan, Carpenter, Casilear & Company, to produce properly.

The stamps were printed from engraved plates of 200 subjects divided into two panes of 100. The individual subjects were far too crowded on the plates. Compounding that, the firm was inexperienced in producing stamps.

Every effort was made to fit the subjects into the plate, but many differences (or types, as they are known to collectors) occurred as a result of alterations of the designs on the relief on the transfer roll (relief trimming), short transfers from insufficient rocking of the relief on the transfer roll, recutting of the design, or erasure.

Thus, on the 1¢ denomination alone, seven major types occur, made more confusing by additional subtypes.

Only one position on the plate of these imperforate issues produced a complete design. This is known as type I. It is the scarcest stamp of this entire issue. Scott catalog lists it at $100,000 unused and $20,000 used.

Type I comes from position 7 on the right pane of Plate I in the early state of the plate (7RIE). This type shows the complete original design: complete right and left ornaments at the top along with the full top line; complete side ornaments; full left and right plumes; left and right balls; and complete bottom line. This type also shows a strong double transfer.

Copies of this stamp are extremely rare because only one position on the plate produced this full design, and in less than a year, the plate was altered and no longer featured a type I subject.

Starting in 1857, the stamps were perforated. Additional plates were made for some values. Plate 12 also produced type I stamps. All are perforated. None shows the double transfer.

The perf stamps also have a secret dot at the left in the white border surrounding the medallion. The imperf type I does not.

The perf stamps are more common than the imperf, and their catalog values reflect this. The perf stamps are listed at $675 unused and $325 used.

Collectors should beware of proofs from the 1875 reprint plate of the type I issues which have been doctored to represent the rare 7RIE position. These also can be identified by the secret dot and lack of double transfer.

Type Ia is a scarce issue. Imperf stamps catalog $13,000 unused and $4,000 used, while perf copies are listed in Scott at $8,500 unused and $2,000 used. This type is the same as type I except that the top ornaments and outer curved frameline at the top are partially cut away. This type occurs only on 18 positions of the bottom row of Plate 4 and can be identified by a small horizontal flaw under the "U." Every type 1a stamp has the flaw, but other types also have it.

Type Ib is the same as type I, but the balls below the bottom scrolls are incomplete.

Type II has the bottoms of the plumes and balls of the scrolls cut away. The top ornaments may or may not be complete, but the top and bottom lines must be complete. This type is within the reach of most collectors, cataloging $450 unused and $85 used for imperf copies; $425 unused and $120 used for perf stamps.

Type III is another scarce stamp. It can be identified by "broken circles," which are breaks in the top and bottom outer curved framelines. These breaks must be distinct to qualify as this type.

Type IIIa is similar to type III, except that either the top or bottom line is broken, but never both.

Type IV is similar to type II, but the curved lines outside the labels have been strengthened by recutting at the top or bottom, or both. This recutting makes the lines appear darker.

Type V is found only on perf stamps. It features broken outer lines similar to type III, but also is identified by the partial cutting away of the side ornaments.

In his book, *The United States One Cent Stamp of 1851 to 1861*, Mortimer Neinken identified two subtypes that the Scott catalog fails to list. Type Ic is the same as type Ia, except that the right plume at the bottom is about half complete, and the right turned under ball at the bottom is only half complete. The left plume is nearly complete. The left ball may be complete or half complete, and may or may not have the flaw under the "U."

Type Va has broken outside curved framelines at the top and bottom. The right ornaments are nearly complete; the left ornaments are incomplete, but more normal than those of type V.

Since the various types of this issue can mean the difference between a common stamp and a great rarity, it is a good idea to have stamps of this series expertized.

Collectors should not be frightened of this issue. Rather, they should be intrigued by it. The 1851 imperf 1¢ blue and its perf counterpart offer many challenges.

UNITED STATES

The Brick Red Jefferson

VALUE: $135,000

Only one unused block of four of the 1857-61 5¢ brick red Jefferson stamp exists, even though it has been estimated that more than 135,000 were issued.

Although the United States 5¢ brick red type I of the 1857-61 series is expensive in any multiple, a one-of-a-kind block of four outshines all other examples of this stamp.

The 5¢ stamps of this series, featuring the portrait of Thomas Jefferson, exist in two major types, and in various shades of red or brown. Type I has projections on all four sides. On type II stamps, the projections at top and bottom are partly cut away. The brick red stamp exists only in Type I

For many years, it was believed the 5¢ brick red, listed in Scott catalog as No. 27, was the first 5¢ stamp issued in the 1857-61 series. However, it is now known that the 5¢ red brown and 5¢ Indian red preceded the brick red stamp by several months.

The earliest known use of the brick red stamp is October 6, 1858. The earliest date for the red brown issue is August 23, 1857. March 31, 1858, is the earliest date for the Indian red stamp. In Lester G. Brookman's *The United States Postage Stamps of the 19th Century*, he estimated the number issued of the 5¢ brick red at 135,000.

The one-of-a-kind unused block of four was part of the Worthington collection when it was sold in 1917 to Arthur Hind. The block also once was part of the Sinkler collection. This rare block realized $135,000 at the Siegel Rarities auction in 1983.

UNITED STATES

A Wartime Provisional

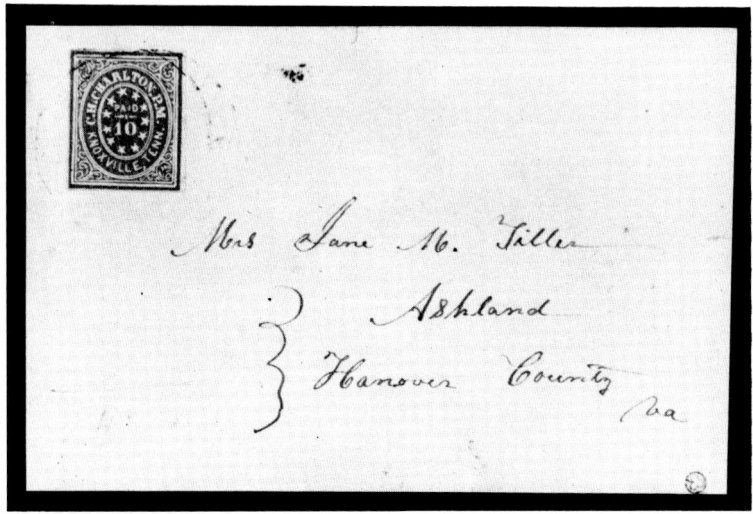

VALUE: $17,500

Only known cover bearing the 10¢ Knoxville, Tennessee, provisional.

The postmasters' provisionals of the Confederate States of America recall a tragic period when the South suffered from many shortages, including coins and postage stamps. By mutual agreement, postal services between the North and South were discontinued on May 31, 1861.

As of June 1, the Confederacy was on its own so far as moving the mails and issuing stamps were concerned. No United States stamps were to be used for prepayment of postage. However, it was impossible for the Confederate Post Office Department to have stamps printed quickly enough. Adhesive stamps were not available until October.

During the interim period, Confederate Postmaster General John H. Reagan advised his postmasters to get along as best they could under such difficult circumstances. A shortage of coins compounded the problem. Customers paid postmasters with Confederate States Treasury notes, but the postmasters often had no coins with which to make change.

The innovative Confederate postmasters devised their own solutions to the problem. Some handstamped the envelopes "Paid." Others issued their own provisional stamps rather than have customers pay for individual letters and risk the chance of the post office not having the necessary coins for change. In this way, the difference could be made up in postage stamps with little or no need for the scarce coins.

Most of these postmasters' provisionals were crudely printed — another sign of the times. Today, however, collectors eagerly seek these crude provisionals. Many are very expensive.

One of the finest covers of this period bears one of the provisional stamps created by C.H. Charlton, postmaster of Knoxville, Tennessee. This is the only cover ever discovered bearing the 10¢ Knoxville provisional stamp.

Such great philatelists as Count Ferrari and Josiah Lilly once owned this cover, which now is in the collection of Scott Gallagher. The Scott *Specialized Catalogue of United States Postage Stamps* lists the cover at $17,500.

Charlton created two 5¢ stamps and one 10¢, along with typographed and handstamped envelopes in the same denominations. The Knoxville provisionals were more sophisticated in design than many of the other Confederate provisionals.

They bear a striking resemblance to the Nashville, Tennessee, and Athens, Georgia, provisionals. It is likely these were engraved by the same person. The stamps were made as woodcuts and printed on grayish laid paper.

Although the 10¢ cover is by far the scarcest item of the Knoxville provisionals, the singles and covers bearing the other denominations are by no means inexpensive. Scott catalog prices range from $650 to $7,000 for these.

UNITED STATES

Essays or Stamps?

VALUE: $35,000

The 12¢ value is the scarcest of the misnamed "August" stamp issues.

Few issues of the United States have generated more confusion and discussion than the so-called "August issues" or *premieres gravures* of 1861. Are these essays or regular stamps?

At one time, collectors believed them to be regular stamps, but now it is generally agreed that they are essays — except for the 10¢ denomination which saw regular use.

In 1861 the United States was in turmoil. On April 12, P.G.T. Beauregard ordered his Confederate troops to fire on Fort Sumter, setting off the Civil War. In the midst of the hostilities, the U.S. Post Office Department became concerned with government-issued postage stamps falling into the hands of the disloyal postmasters of the Confederacy. The Post Office demonetized its current stamps to prevent fraudulent use.

The contract for printing stamps was up for renewal, so it was a logical time to change the designs. The new stamps would be easily recognized by their design and would discourage the use of the demonetized issues.

The National Bank Note Company submitted the lowest printing bid to the USPOD, nudging out the former printer, Toppan, Carpenter and Company.

With a new printer and new stamp designs, the USPOD decided to take this opportunity to tighten its control over its postal issues. The post office demanded that each printer submit specimens to be approved by a board of experts. The successful bidder was required to furnish "proof impressions of the engravings of the several denominations of stamps."

The sample designs, or essays, submitted by the National Bank Note Company are now known as the *premieres gravures* (first engravings) or "August issues." These issues can be identified by their brittle, transparent paper and dark gum, as well as by distinguishing marks in the frames of some values.

The designs feature portraits of Benjamin Franklin, George Washington and Thomas Jefferson. The denominations and colors are 1¢ indigo, 3¢ brown rose, 5¢ brown, 10¢ dark green, 12¢ black, 24¢ dark violet, 30¢ red orange, and 90¢ dull blue.

How did these issues gain catalog status as regular stamps? One reason is that several copies turned up in Europe, and many collectors felt this to be proof that the issues were meant for and used as postage stamps. However, they probably were sent as samples that were not intended for use.

The *premieres gravures* continue to be listed along with the regular issues in most catalogs, although most collectors today agree they are essays or trial color proofs. The one exception is the 10¢ issue, which actually saw use along with the 1861 10¢ yellow green regular issue.

Most philatelists agree that the 24¢ and 30¢ are trial color proofs submitted to the USPOD along with the National Bank Note Company's bid, as required by bidding rules.

The nickname "August issues" also is a misnomer. Some collectors referred to the essays as August issues to distinguish them from the regular issues which they believed were released in September. However, many of the regular stamps made their debut in August, not September.

The *premieres gravures* continue to fascinate collectors who consider them to be among the true gems of U.S. philately. Their catalog prices reflect their scarcity. The 12¢ black is the scarcest and catalogs at $35,000 in Scott. The 3¢ is the most common, cataloging at $700. Other values range from $4,750 for the 10¢ to $19,000 for the 90¢ denominations.

UNITED STATES

A Cajun Rarity

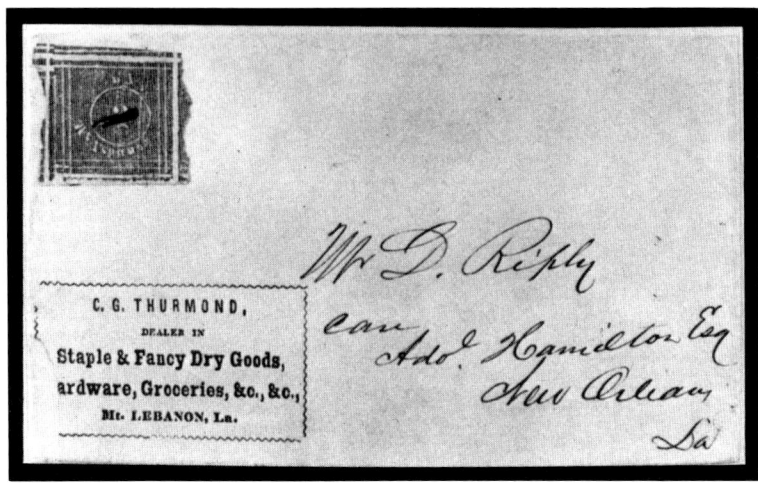

VALUE: $50,000

Only this copy of the Mount Lebanon postmaster's provisional is known.

Several postmasters' provisional issues of the Confederate States of America are scarce, but only one Mt. Lebanon, Louisiana, 5¢ red brown exists. This copy is on a cover addressed to Mr. D. Riply in New Orleans, Louisiana. The provisional is most unusual in that the design is reversed — a mirror image.

The stamp is affixed to the upper left-hand corner of the cover. In the lower left-hand corner appears the corner card of C.G. Thurmond, a dealer in "Staple & Fancy Dry Goods,/Hardware, Groceries, &c.,&c.," in Mt. Lebanon.

Beginning June 1, 1861, United States stamps no longer were permitted to be used as postage in the Southern states which had seceded. Many of the postmasters in the Confederate States issued their own provisional stamps and postal stationery to be used in the interim period until the CSA post office issued its own stamps October 16, 1861.

The postmaster of Mt. Lebanon issued only one stamp — a 5¢ denomination produced from a woodcut. The urgency with which this stamp was printed is evidenced by the fact that the image is reversed. The printer obviously knew little about printing and the steps necessary to produce a proper vignette.

The letters in printer's type are reversed. The printer of the Mt. Lebanon provisional hammered his type face down into a block of wood producing indented lettering. However, he forgot that since the lettering was normal on the woodcut, it would appear reversed when the stamps were printed.

The cover bearing the unique provisional once was owned by the famous French collector, Count Ferrari, who formed an impressive collection of the Confederate provisionals. Alfred Caspary, an equally famous collector who lived in the United States, purchased the cover at the Ferrari sales following World War I.

This rarity once again was sold when H.R. Harmer Company auctioned the Caspary collection in 1956. It realized $5,500. Charles E. Kilbourne later bought the Mt. Lebanon provisional, adding this unique cover to his great collection of the Confederate States.

Today, the Scott *Specialized Catalogue of United States Stamps* lists the Mt. Lebanon provisional at $50,000.

UNITED STATES

The One and Only Pair

VALUE: $176,000

A pair of the Livingston postmaster's provisional, the only known multiple still intact, is on a homemade cover to Manassas Junction, Virginia.

The "aristocrat of Confederate covers." The "most artistic" of all Confederate provisionals. A "rebel rarity." These are only some of the titles which have been applied to the famous cover bearing a pair of the Livingston Confederate provisional.

On June 18, 1985, this one-of-a-kind cover realized a record $176,000, including a 10 percent buyer's premium, when auctioned by Christie's/Robson Lowe in New York City. The cover returned home to its former owners, the Weill brothers of New Orleans.

Stephen W. Murley, postmaster of Livingston, Alabama, during the Civil War, issued this 5¢ stamp in 1861. Southern states which had seceded from the Union no longer were permitted to use United States stamps, and stamps of the Confederate States of America were not yet available. Several postmasters issued their own stamps for the interim period.

However, most of these were crudely designed and produced.

Compared to other Confederate provisionals, Murley's Livingston stamp is an artistic masterpiece. It features a shaded numeral "5" on a shield as its central design. Eleven stars on the shield represent the 11 Confederate States. It also features three stripes. Laurel leaves surround the shield which is topped by a shining star. Tiny cherub faces peer at the shield from each corner.

The Livingston provisional in itself is a great rarity. A single is listed in Scott catalog at $8,000. The stamp on cover catalogs at $35,000.

An employee of a Southern railroad discovered two singles on cover about 1869. The stamps were removed from the cover. One was sold to Francis Foster, a Massachusetts collector, for a mere $7. A Dr. Petrie bought the other for about $20. The discovery of this cover was first reported in Volume 3 of the *American Stamp Mercury* in 1869.

But the gem of this issue is the cover bearing a pair, the only known multiple of the Livingston provisional intact. Tracing the discovery of this item is more difficult. The homemade envelope is addressed to "Capt. R. Chapman, Jr./11th Reg't Ala. Vol./Manassas Junction/Va./Care of/Col. Syd. Moore." The pair of stamps is tied by a Livingston Nov. 12 (1861) datestamp.

French collector Count Ferrari added this rarity to his remarkable collection of Confederate material in the late 1800's. Who owned the cover prior to this is a mystery. It is possible Ferrari bought it from U.S. stamp dealer Charles H. Mekeel, who sold the count many Confederate items.

Warren Colson paid 22,000 francs for the cover at the Ferrari sales following World War I. He was acting as Alfred Caspary's agent. When the Caspary Confederate collection was sold in 1956 by H.R. Harmer, Raymond and Robert Weill paid $14,000 for the Livingston cover, a record realization for a Confederate item at that time.

Josiah K. Lilly, a famous U.S. collector and pharmaceutical magnate, bought the cover to add to his fabulous worldwide collection. When the Lilly collection was sold by Robert A. Siegel Auction Galleries in 1967, John R. Boker Jr. paid $19,000 for the Livingston gem. A collector in Europe later bought the cover from Boker in a private sale.

But now the "aristocrat of Confederate covers" has returned to New Orleans after achieving a record price of $176,000.

UNITED STATES

No "Z" in Z Grills

VALUE: $110,000
One of only two copies of the 1¢ blue
"Z" grill U.S. stamp known to exist.

Among the most complex issues of United States stamps are its early grilled stamps. An ability to identify the various grills can mean the difference between a relatively inexpensive stamp and one worth more than $100,000.

Of all the grilled stamps, the scarcest and most expensive is the 1867 1¢ blue "Z" grill. Only two copies exist — one used, the other unused. Scott catalog lists the used stamp at $110,000 but gives no price for the unused copy.

But don't start searching through your 1867 stamps for one with a grill in the form of a "Z". The letter has nothing to do with the shape of the grill. Grills were the patented idea of Charles F. Steel. They consisted of waffle-like embossed designs impressed into the printed stamps.

Although it is uncertain exactly how these grills were placed on the stamps, it is believed they were made by male and female rollers. The male roller consisted of tiny raised pyramids; the female roller consisted of tiny depressions.

When the male roller penetrated the front of the stamp, forcing the paper into the female roller, a points down grill resulted. When the male roller penetrated the back of the stamp, forcing the face into the female roller, a points up grill occurred.

The purpose of the grills was to prevent unscrupulous individuals from removing cancellations and reusing stamps. The pyramids broke the paper fiber, and the canceling ink soaked into the paper, thus preventing removal of the cancellation.

The letters assigned to the grills had nothing to do with their shape. William Stevenson, a prominent collector, assigned the letter "A" to the largest grill, "B" to the second largest, and continued through the letter "J."

However, a curious grill made its appearance. While all other grills have short vertical tips, those of the "Z" grill type are horizontal. In other words, the paper on the "Z" grill issue is broken horizontally rather than vertically.

The "Z" grill stumped Stevenson. He was undecided about the letter to assign to it. Finally, he decided upon the letter "Z" and inserted it between the "D" and "E" grills. "A" through "C" grills are female; "D" through "J," including the "Z," are male.

All stamps with "Z" grills are scarce. They have been found on the 1¢ blue, 2¢ black, 3¢ rose, 10¢ green, 12¢ black and 15¢ black of the 1867 series. The grill measures 13 by 14 millimeters (13-14 by 17-18 points). Scott lists the 1¢ at $110,000 used; 2¢, $900 unused, $275 used; 3¢, $2,500 unused, $750 used; 10¢, $23,500 unused; 12¢, $1,350 unused, $475 used; and 15¢, $35,000 used.

In 1977 a used 1¢ "Z" grill set what was at that time a world record for the highest auction realization by any American stamp — $90,000. This was paid by Superior Stamp and Coin Company at the May 25, 1977 Sotheby Parke Bernet sale in New York.

Saul Newbury, the prominent collector of 19th century U.S. and other issues of the world, was unaware that he owned a copy of the 15¢ "Z" grill for many years. He had misidentified it. So, some "Z" grills are attainable; others are great rarities. If you think you've discovered one among your stamps, have it expertized.

UNITED STATES

But 80 Percent Are Fakes

VALUE: $115,000

The National Bank Note Company produced this rare U.S. 24¢ grill. Only three unused copies exist.

Among the rarest unused United States stamps is the 1870 24¢ grill produced by the National Bank Note Company. Used specimens also are scarce, since only 2,000 grill stamps were printed.

So your chances of discovering a 24¢ grill are slim at best — at least chances of discovering a genuine copy. The prospects of coming across this issue with a fake grill, however, are good.

Peter Robertson, curator of the Philatelic Foundation, says 80 percent of the 24¢ grill stamps submitted to the Foundation for expertizing have fake grills.

Yet, despite the high percentage of fakes, collectors continue to search for these elusive stamps. And why not? After all, it's the dream of finding a rarity that makes stamp collecting exciting.

Only three unused copies of the 24¢ grill exist. One is in the Thomas Tapling collection in the British Museum. Another copy gained fame as part of the Miller collection stolen from the New York City Public Library. That stamp recently was recovered.

Superior Stamp and Coin Galleries auctioned the third copy in its October 29-31, 1984 sale of the Pepperdine University collection. The stamp realized $115,000, a price attesting to this issue's rarity in unused condition. Used copies of the 24¢ grill catalog in Scott at $10,500, so even the genuine used copies are extremely valuable.

By contrast, used copies of the 24¢ without the grill catalog at $70. Thus you can see why unscrupulous persons add their fake grills to these stamps.

In 1870 U.S. Postmaster General John A.J. Creswell adopted the designs of the U.S. Bank Note issues to replace the prior 1869 pictorial issues. The Bank Notes, so-called because they were printed by the National Bank Note Company, Continental Bank Note Company, and American Bank Note Company, feature profiles of distinguished deceased Americans.

The 24¢ portrays General Winfield Scott, an American army officer who served in the War of 1812, Mexican War, and Civil War. The stamp is printed in purple, but most copies found today are faded. NBNC printed 2,000 24¢ stamps with the grill.

Grills were the patented idea of Charles F. Steel. They consist of waffle-like embossed designs applied to printed stamps to prevent people from removing cancellations and reusing the stamps. The pyramids of the grills broke the paper fiber, and the canceling ink soaked into the paper, making it impossible to remove.

The NBNC produced 1,148,000 of the 24¢ denomination without grills, so there are plenty of stamps available to which grills can be added. The 24¢ grills on cover are particularly suspect. The genuine stamp is extremely rare on cover.

Since collectors are reluctant to remove a stamp from a cover to check the grill, fakers frequently remove a 24¢ without grill from a cover, add a fake grill, replace it on the cover, and offer it as a genuine grill copy.

For this reason, collectors should have all 24¢ grills expertized before buying them. A certificate of authenticity will only enhance such a philatelic treasure.

UNITED STATES

The Precious Persian Rug

VALUE: $15,000

The 1871 $500 United States revenue stamp is known as the "Persian Rug," because its design suggests the appearance of such a carpet.

The "Persian Rug" revenue of the United States intrigues collectors. Where did it get its name? Why such a high denomination? What makes it so rare? This $500 revenue stamp made its debut in 1871 as part of the second issue of U.S. Internal Revenue stamps.

Collectors nicknamed it the "Persian Rug," both because of its enormous size (engraving measures 52 millimeters by 100mm) and the intricately engraved lathework resembling a Persian rug. The stamp features a Gilbert Stuart portrait of George Washington.

The Persian Rug was printed in black, green and red on a special security paper known as chameleon paper. The paper contained a chemical coloring which changed or faded if an acid or alkali was used to clean the stamp to remove the cancellation.

The high denomination of $500 was needed for documents covering transactions which required taxes of $500 or more. A transaction for such a large sum of money was rare in the 1870's, accounting for the stamp's scarcity. Only 204 were printed.

In his March 6, 1954 "Sloane's Column" in *Stamps*, George B. Sloane, a famous philatelic writer, called attention to an extraordinary revenue mortgage document for $5 million bearing ten copies of the $500 Persian Rug along with a 25¢ revenue.

Each stamp on this document is canceled in manuscript, "Hoboken, Oct. 2/71. Fred R. Chambers, Secretary, M. and E.R.R. Co." The mortgage papers were executed for the Morris and Essex Railroad, a New Jersey line.

The Persian Rug seldom comes up for sale at auction. When it does, it achieves high realizations. Scott catalog lists it at $15,000.

UNITED STATES

An Erroneous Columbian

VALUE: $6,500

Is the 4¢ blue 1893 Columbian an error of color or a shade variety? Most experts agree it is a color error.

Is the United States 4¢ blue Columbian an error of color or a shade variety? Collectors have argued this point for years. With the high prices the stamp has realized, it can be concluded that most collectors agree the stamp is an error of color.

Today, collectors eagerly seek copies of the Columbians to add to their albums, finding that many of the sound stamps are beyond their financial reach. However, collectors once looked disdainfully upon this lengthy commemorative issue.

The Columbians made their debut in 1893, coinciding with the World's Columbian Exposition in Chicago. The year-late exposition celebrated the 400th anniversary of the discovery of the New World by Christopher Columbus, and the 16 stamps pictured important incidents in Columbus' life.

Stamp collectors felt such a wide roster of 16 denominations (1¢ to $5) was aimed at their pocketbooks. They responded by refusing to buy the issue. Those who did purchase Columbians found they had little resale value at first.

One stamp in this series always has intrigued collectors — the 4¢ blue. The normal 4¢ denomination is printed in ultramarine.

The question has been raised again and again: Was this an error of color or a shade variety? To further complicate matters, two shades of the color error have been discovered.

For years, collectors were aware of dark dull blue 4¢ color error stamps, although little is known of their provenance.

However, in the late 1970's, another color came on the market. These later discoveries are now described simply as blue, while the others are referred to as a darker duller blue.

Of course, collectors questioned the blue error. When a 4¢ blue was submitted to the Philatelic Foundation for expertizing, it created quite a stir. The experts were suspicious.

So, the stamp was subjected to scientific tests, but it was concluded to be a genuine error. No traces of ultramarine were found in the ink, thereby dispelling forever the idea that it was nothing but a chemical changeling.

In September 1893, J.V. Painter, a collector in Cleveland, purchased a sheet of the 4¢ Columbian. He immediately noticed the striking difference between the color of this sheet and the normal stamp. The sheet was from Plate D17. Painter broke up the sheet, selling copies to his fellow collectors.

Some collectors speculated that the 4¢ had been printed in the blue ink of the 1¢. Others argued that the color was too rich to be compared with the 1¢. Today, it is generally agreed that the stamp is an error of color and not a shade variety, but no one is certain how the error occurred.

The American Bank Note Company printed the Columbians, the last issue of the 19th century to be produced by a private firm. It is possible that the printer started printing the 4¢ stamps with the ultramarine ink, and when the ink ran out, he mistakenly replaced it with the blue. When he discovered his error, he replaced the blue ink with the correct ultramarine.

The 4¢ blue Columbians are scarce; Scott catalog lists them at $6,500 unused and $2,500 used.

Although the Columbians failed to gain collector interest in the 19th century, they have earned the respect of collectors in the 20th century. So much so, that many find the superior quality stamps priced well out of their reach.

UNITED STATES

Garbage Collector's Gem

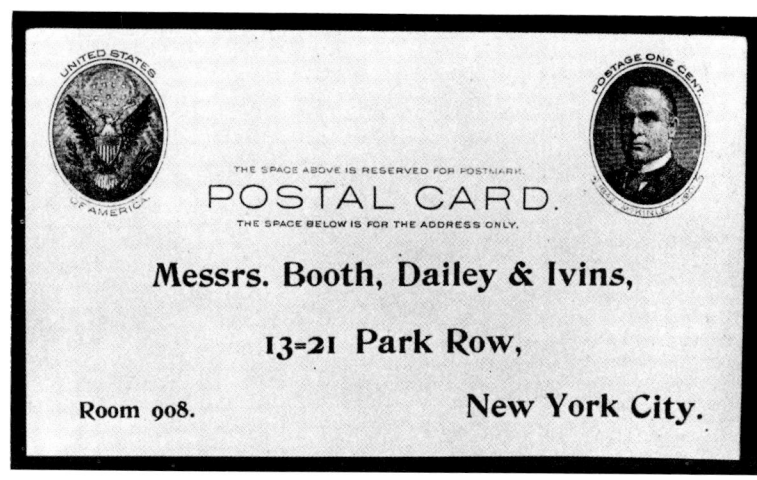

VALUE: $3,000

Only 500 of these scarce full-face McKinley cards escaped postal destruction. They are known as the "garbage cards," because all were used by the Booth, Dailey & Ivins Company, a firm which held the exclusive contract for dumping all of New York City's garbage at sea.

    The gem of United States postal cards, the 1902 1¢ full-face McKinley, carries the unattractive nickname "garbage card." Most collectors prefer to ignore this term. The nickname is not a reflection on the design or the card itself. Rather, it came about because most of the cards were used by a garbage collector.

    In 1901 an assassin gunned down U.S. President William McKinley at the Pan-American Exposition in Buffalo, New York. The public flooded the U.S. Post Office Department with requests for a memorial stamp to honor their fallen president. However, their supplications fell on deaf ears.

    As a compromise, the USPOD decided to honor McKinley with a 1¢ postal card. Unfortunately, the contract for printing this card was given to Albert Daggett, who was known for his inferior work.

Daggett produced specimens featuring a full-face portrait of McKinley. He sent these to the USPOD for authorization. Even so, Daggett's high-speed presses failed to produce a suitable design. Also, it is said that McKinley's widow hated the portrait.

The USPOD, therefore, rejected the design, and Postmaster General Henry C. Payne ordered the entire expensive stock of the 1,625,000 cards destroyed.

A box of 500 somehow slipped out. This box was shipped to New York City and sold by the New York City Post Office to Booth, Dailey and Ivins, a company which held the city contract for dumping garbage at sea. The company imprinted each card "Messrs. Booth, Dailey and Ivins,/13-21 Park Row,/New York City" on the front. In the lower left was "Room 908."

A form was printed on the back of the card. Barge tenders had to fill out this form, which served as a record of each day's business. Thus, the nickname, "garbage card." The earliest known use of the card was May 27, 1902.

All 500 cards were addressed, so none of the full-face McKinleys properly issued by the USPOD is known in mint condition. ("Mint," in the lexicon of the postal card collector, means a card which is both uncanceled and unaddressed.)

R.H. Lamscha, a stamp collector, was the first to notice the use of these rare postal cards. At first, he thought they must have mysteriously escaped destruction by the post office. Then he noticed the address of the garbage collector. He immediately wrote to the company, enclosing 5¢ and asking that they send him a sample, which they did. He then contacted several dealers to show them the cards. He sold a card to Scott Stamp and Coin Company, but he had erased the address from this card.

J. Murray Bartels asked Lamscha to negotiate a deal with the garbage company for the remaining cards. Lamscha not only bought 312 of the cards used by the company, but also 149 unused cards. Thirty-eight used cards never have been found.

Bartels later sold his remaining stock to Siegfried Schachne, a postal stationery dealer in Chillicothe, Ohio. Some years later, Schachne sold his remaining stock to Dr. Walton I. Mitchell of Berkley, California. It is believed that Dr. Mitchell lost most of his stock in a fire. Unused cards are those which carry the company name and form, but were never used. These differ from mint cards which are in post office condition and carry no additional printing.

The only "mint" cards known to exist were taken from production during an inspection. However, these must be regarded as specimens because they never were issued by the post office.

According to the United Postal Stationery Society's *United States Postal Card Catalog*, more unused cards now exist than used. But prices do not reflect this. Unused cards usually sell for more than used cards. The Scott U.S. Specialized lists the full-face McKinley at $5,000 mint, $3,000 unused and $2,500 used.

URUGUAY

Ferrari's Crayon Error

VALUE: $7,500 plus
The 180c dull vermilion color error of Uruguay was created when a cliche of the 180c was mistakenly placed in the stone for the 240c.

Stamp collectors share a camaraderie seldom experienced by others. Many great philatelists have helped new collectors on their way by trading duplicates or giving advice. Collectors seldom forget those who have helped them find an elusive stamp or cover.

Charles J. Phillips, a distinguished philatelist and dealer, frequently told a story illustrating such camaraderie. It involved the rare Uruguay 180-centavo vermilion error of color.

Phillips said the renowned French collector, Count Ferrari, took a special interest in two brothers, Georges and Montoil Caillebotte.

He helped them build their collections by giving them duplicates from his extensive worldwide collection. Ferrari also advised the brothers in their acquisitions of new stamps for their collection.

Most collectors are familiar with the stories about Ferrari's attempts to assemble one of every stamp in the world. But the Caillebotte brothers had one stamp Ferrari had not yet obtained — the Uruguay error of color.

In March 1858, Uruguay issued a set of three stamps. From this set came Uruguay's three great rarities — the tete-beche pairs of the 120c and 180c, and the 180c dull vermilion error of color. The color error occurred when the cliche of the 180c was mistakenly placed in the stone of the 240c dull vermilion, resulting in an 180c dull vermilion. Normal copies of this value are printed in green. The cliche later was removed, leaving a blank space.

Stanley Gibbons refuses to list the error in its catalog. The Gibbons South America specialized catalog states: "We no longer list the error 180c red from the stone of the 240c as there is considerable doubt as to whether a genuine copy exists. It is believed that any known copies are normal 180c stamps with the color chemically changed." Scott catalog lists the error but gives no price.

Only one genuine copy of the error exists, although fakes have come onto the market. The genuine copy is defective. In addition to other faults, it has a piece missing at left.

It is not surprising that Ferrari wanted to add this one-of-a-kind stamp to his collection. When the Caillebottes finally decided to sell their collection, they remembered their dear friend who had helped them develop their love for philately. Before they sold the collection to Thomas Kay Tapling, they removed the Uruguay 180c color error. It was sold to Ferrari.

At the auctions of the Ferrari collections in 1921, his Uruguay collection was sold intact as one lot to Alfred F. Lichtenstein. Lichtenstein exhibited it at the international exhibition in New York in 1926 and captured the grand award. On his death, he bequeathed the error to his daughter, Louise Boyd Dale.

At the Dale-Lichtenstein auction conducted by H.R. Harmer May 7, 1970, John R. Boker Jr. paid $7,500 for the 180c color error. Boker says when he bought the stamp, it was pasted to the original Ferrari brownish paper mounting and crudely marked with red crayon to reduce the missing portion of the stamp. Boker traded the rarity to a dealer for other classics. Dr. Norman Hubbard later bought the stamp and is its current owner.

So Why Imperforate?

VALUE: $22,500

Why the imperforate stamps of Vancouver Island were even produced is a mystery to collectors.

Vancouver Island, located off the northwest coast of Canada, issued four stamps bearing only the island's name with no mention of British Columbia. One of these — the imperforate 5¢ — is a great rarity.

Philatelists have long been unfair to Vancouver Island. They join the island with British Columbia, even though Vancouver operated its own postal service separate from British Columbia for several years. The confusion stems from an 1860 issue bearing the names of both British Columbia and Vancouver Island. Revenues from the sale of these stamps, however, were appropriately divided between the two colonies.

Vancouver Island was a thriving colony during the gold rush of the 1860's. But when the miners ceased traveling through the colony, the economy collapsed. The country was at its lowest financial point in 1865 when Vancouver issued its first stamps carrying only the name of the island.

Thomas De La Rue in England printed and shipped 114,000 5¢ rose and 111,360 10¢ blue stamps to the island. Most of these were perforated 14. But for some unknown reason, a small number of imperforate stamps in both values were included in the shipment. Philatelists are uncertain whether these imperforates were errors or deliberate issues. Regardless, the imperforates are scarce, particularly the 5¢.

Mint copies of this denomination rank among the great rarities of the world. Scott catalog prices them at $22,500 mint and $4,250 used. The imperforate 10¢ is listed at $1,250 mint and $725 used.

To further add to the confusion of the Vancouver Island and British Columbia stamps, the Vancouver stamps were in use only a short time before the two colonies merged. The remainders of the Vancouver stamps were transferred to the postmaster general of the united colony for general usage.

In his book, *The Colonial Postal Systems and Postage Stamps of Vancouver Island and British Columbia 1849-1871*, Alfred Stanley Deaville says that only 39,900 5¢ and 1,200 10¢ stamps were used by Vancouver during its separate existence. How many of these were produced imperforate is unknown.